TIMES OF HEALTH AND CONSCIENTIOUSNESS

DIVALDO FRANCO
BY THE SPIRIT JOANNA DE ÂNGELIS

TIMES OF HEALTH AND CONSCIENTIOUSNESS

LEAL Publisher

ISBN: 978-1-942408-96-3

Original title in Portuguese:
Momentos de Saúde e de Consciência
(Brazil, 1991)

Translated by: Darrel W. Kimble and Claudia Dealmeida
Cover design by: Cláudio Urpia
Layout: Luciano Carneiro Holanda
Edited by: Evelyn Yuri Furuta

Edition of
LEAL PUBLISHER
8425 Biscayne Blvd. Suite 104
Miami, Florida 33138, USA
www.lealpublisher.com
info@lealpublisher.com
(305) 306-6447

Authorized edition by Centro Espírita Caminho da Redenção – Salvador (BA) – Brazil

INTERNATIONAL DATA FOR CATALOGING IN PUBLICATION (ICP)

f825   Ângelis, de Joanna (Spirit).
                 Times of Health and Conscientiousness / authored by the Spirit
             Joanna de Ângelis; psychographed by Divaldo Pereira Franco ; translated
             by Darrel Kimble and Claudia Dealmeida. – Miami (FL), USA : Leal
             Publisher, 2016.

                 173 p. ; 21 cm

                 Original title: Momentos de Saúde e de Consciência

                 ISBN 978-1-942408-96-39

                 1. Spiritism. 2. Psychology. 3. Behavior. 4. Health
             I. Franco, Divaldo Pereira, 1927-. II. Title.
                                                        CDD 133.9
                                                        CDU 133.7

CONTENTS

TIMES OF HEALTH

TIMES OF CONSCIENTIOUSNESS

TIMES OF HEALTH

*B*eing completely healthy is a much-desired goal.
Achieving bodily, emotional and mental harmony in an
overall framework of well-being is a great challenge to
the human mind, which for millennia has sought the most
varied and complex experiences, resulting in remarkable and
invaluable accomplishments.

From that specific endeavor allied with others of
technology-supported science aimed at the environment and
other destructive factors, human life today has reached the
highest rates of longevity ever.

Humans have managed to banish from the earth diseases
that used to decimate entire populations, constantly threatening
the human race with extinction.

Diagnostic accuracy and the use of sophisticated
equipment have achieved the miracle of detecting serious
illnesses either before their calamitous manifestation, or at
their onset. Additionally, advanced therapies prolong physical
existence, decrease pain and preserve the organs, even if they
have become affected.

Of course, new diseases do appear and take over the
human landscape, but they are researched and combated
relentlessly.

People instinctively seek either to avoid suffering altogether or at least to free themselves from it by using all the resources imaginable.

Due to the blessing of the self-preservation instinct, everyone intrinsically fears aging, pain and death, avoiding, as much as possible, acts of extreme despair that end in suicide, that nefarious enemy of the spirit's evolution.

Deriving from their low level of evolution, humans develop lacerating infirmities because they are still the target of health-related ailments and disorders.

As individuals pursue self-discovery and embark on the inner journey aided by self-love, they find that health is an interior acquisition reflected in the body as a result of inner harmony.

Fortunately, medical science has broadened its conceptual catalog regarding health and disease and has begun to include other disciplines that contribute effectively to people's well-being.

The modern findings of psychosomatic medicine have demonstrated that mental and emotional pathologies easily transfer to the body, setting the scene for various diseases. When the energy balance that sustains the cells is disturbed, immunological factors become altered under bombardment by destructive mental discharges, which encourages deadly agents to take root and grow, causing the body to breakdown.

That is why it is imperative to usher in an era of a new awareness of responsibility so that, lucid and balanced, individuals may establish the paradigms for harmonious moral and mental conduct in order to acquire the priceless asset of health.

Throughout the Gospels, Jesus exalts moral and emotional harmony as essential for salvation, that is, a state of complete health.

A unique psychotherapist, He proposes self-examination as a means for acquiring peace by loving God above all things and one's neighbor as oneself.

A synthesis of unparalleled wisdom, love is the key to the illness-health enigma.

Later on, updating the Master's thought, Allan Kardec[1] established charity as the therapy for peace and the model for the correct application of love.

Nowadays, various sciences are in agreement with this, especially transpersonal, transactional and creative psychologies, which propound self-discovery, release from mental and moral rubble, victory over the ego, and the coming to plenitude of the Self, the eternal spiritual I, in its unstoppable process of growth.

Wishing to participate in that blessed effort developed by the "priests" of health, we offer the dear reader this humble contribution. It does not present any innovations, but aims to build a bridge between the outstanding contributions of technical knowledge and the wise teachings of Jesus and Allan Kardec, narrowing the chasm between science per se and religion so that they may advance hand-in-hand, benefiting people and society in their search for a happy tomorrow.

Hoping that these times of health may be the portico to complete health, we feel rewarded by the pleasure of participating in the Lord's work as a minor and dedicated servant.

JOANNA DE ÂNGELIS
Salvador, Brazil, October 22, 1992

---

[1]   Allan Kardec (1804-1869), Codifier of Spiritism. – Tr.

9

Divine Consciousness flows through me.
God sustains and leads me all the days of my life.

*There is an ebb and flow of force that runs through
me and drives me forward.*
*It is up to me to coordinate the activities, choose the
goal and move ahead.*

*Submitting myself to that life force, everything
becomes accessible to me, and I can reach the
fruition of my aspirations in peace.*

1
DECIDING TO BE HAPPY

D o your best to make your life pleasant for yourself and others.

It is important that everything you do has a positive meaning, that it provides new stimuli for you to continue your life, which ought to be characterized by enriching experiences.

If the people around you do not comply with your decision to be happy, do not get discouraged; peacefully continue generating well-being.

You yourself are the only person you can count on to always be with you from cradle to grave and thereafter, as a result of your acts...

Generating affinity while providing yourself with optimistic stimuli points to significant emotional growth, to psychological maturity in full bloom.

It is important for your behavior to produce agreeable, kindly exchanges with others. However, if you find such exchanges unpleasant they become a torment, causing you to harbor perturbing, dishonest attitudes.

Your changes and demeanor affect those you live with, so it is natural that, in fulfilling yourself, such changes and demeanor foster more resources for generating cheerfulness all around you.

✳

All the great leaders of humanity have struggled until they reached their goal – attaining what they had chosen as happiness, as central for their ongoing search.

Buddha renounced all the comforts of being a prince to attain enlightenment.

Muhammad suffered persecution, yet remained indomitable until he achieved his goal.

Gandhi was arrested many times but did not fight back. He stayed faithful to his plans of non-violence and freedom for his people.

And Jesus chose the infamous cross rather than change His love-based behavior.

All those who long to become one with Cosmic Consciousness generate both affinity and animosity. They are always dealing with other people's opposite sentiments. Even so, they stay true to themselves. They know they can always count on themselves, and God, of course.

✳

Those who choose a life enriched with peace and well-being are not trying to get out of suffering, struggling and difficulties. On the contrary, these always appear as perturbing challenges, which individuals must face without losing their way or altering the pleasure they experience in preserving their chosen behavior. So, dear reader, transform your painful stimuli into positive contributions, and do not complain, suffer or give up.

Those who see only suffering in the struggle have a pathological problem that needs appropriate treatment.

Life is a blessing and should be kept healthy, cheerful and promising, even when under the liberating imperative of trials and expiations.

If you make your life enjoyable, all your days will be fruitful and sunny.

*The Divine Thought has given me the
freedom to accomplish all the good that I desire.*

Being happy or unhappy is my free choice.

*I am slave to the Law, which enables me to
progress without stopping.*

What I am or what I will be depends on me.

*Inspiration from above is never lacking;
however, attuning myself to it shall be my
personal aspiration.*

*Erecting existential structures in my mind, I
shall make them a reality over the course of my
life.*

2
FREEDOM OF CHOICE

You are free to mark your life with the standard of happiness or affliction with which you want to live. Freedom is a Law of Life, and is part of the concert of universal harmony.

The immovable, deterministic imperatives concerning the physical body are life and death, although even these two aspects are subject to the fatalism of incessant change.

Subject to actions, which, in turn, trigger corresponding reactions, you are what you make of yourself on your chosen pathway.

There are people who prefer to gripe and complain, storing up self-serving pessimism. They use their large number of mentally created ailments to *barter* for love.

Others adopt imagined sufferings to *blackmail* their loved ones for attention and physical affection. However, such attention is never enough for them. They do not realize that what they are doing will only dry up the generous supply offered to them.

Nobody feels good among people who use misfortune as a false solution to their existential conflicts.

This emotional duress ends up producing false friendships, embarrassing situations, and more insecurity.

✳

You can and should be happy. It is your free choice.

If you find yourself pulling a wagon of woes, strive to do the good and you will unhitch yourself from it.

The difficulty of today is the effect of the folly of the past.

Life is renewed at every moment.

Dire situations change for the better, like shadow-filled landscapes suddenly lit by the sun.

Do not make a truce with misfortune, idleness or complaining.

You are the master of your destiny, and its meeting point for you is the infinite.

Those who devalue, discredit and invalidate themselves get left behind.

It is imperative that you get positively *involved* with the Divine Plan; those who do not, never grow.

If you would rather suffer, you are free to do so until you finally opt for well-being.

So, do not make mountains out of mole hills.

No one is destined to suffer. Suffering is always the result of a negative action, never the cause.

✳

Without a guilty conscience, sentimentality or coercion, make an honest evaluation of your life and awaken to what you should produce that is good, useful and constructive, fully invested in your happiness.

The Divine Presence supports me in the processes of growth and renewal.

Every moment is another opportunity for me to advance or to correct my mistakes.

The transformations that life brings about are stages of development.

Pruning renews; pain awakens; a trial educates; a change in behavior requires effort.

Because I am a child of God, I am destined for happiness, a goal I will reach through renewal and struggle.

3
RENEWAL

L ife is a continual dynamic of transformation. Nothing remains unchanged. Change is a natural phenomenon of the renewing process. Whatever is not renewed dies; this is a fact of evolution. Repose is a misinterpretation of undetected occurrences.

Thus, the emotions, the physical body, and human behavior are all subject to the imperatives of necessary changes, which vary according to the circumstances.

These changes in the human being derive from different states of consciousness, various mental patterns, and different philosophies about life.

As you think, so you proceed.

The mind, externalizing its psychological levels, is responsible for the attitudes by which people express their individual spiritual reality.

The process that precedes an action is mental in nature. Therefore, all that is mentally affirmed or denied exerts a preponderance that *materializes* in the field of objective reality.

Cultivating pessimistic ideas, which generate infirmities, troubles, sorrows and tragedies, must be replaced by healthy, productive thoughts, responsible for the goods things in life.

No one is doomed to misery. By renewing yourself, you change your landscape for the future, according to what you prepare in the area of your mental desires.

*

Your thoughts follow in the direction of your aspirations; that is, what you long for emotionally, you construct mentally. Thus, you will succeed according to your wishes.

Of course, throughout your physical existence you will endure trials and expiations arising from past thoughts and attitudes that are now catching up with you now as mechanisms of reparation, redemption and reeducation.

If you had acted differently in the past, you would be facing different karmic situations in the present.

Despite such effects, the Law of Renewal pushes you to modify the structure of forthcoming days by means of today's conduct.

Review your action plan as soon as possible. Submit it to a composed analysis and ponder your current possibilities, reworking projects and setting new goals.

If your plan seems correct, expand it. If it seems insufficient or troublesome, fix it. But renew yourself, continuously changing for the better your willingness to grow regardless of the circumstances.

*

Do not require that people be like you, that they remain unchanged, with the same old habits, expressing the same feelings in relation to you.

When faced with affections that have decreased in intensity; behaviors and situations that have changed; friends who have made new choices; enthusiasm that has cooled or shifted elsewhere; and new challenges, do not rebel through depression or violence. Such are the changes imposed by life. Accept them calmly and peacefully, continuing with your lofty ideals and always evolving, without ties to the rearguard or anxiety about the future.

Divine Force pervades my mind and body.

I have been reborn into a painful situation as a lesson for my evolution.

People are as they please, but I am on a perennial search for harmony.

The evil others have done to me will become an asset.

*It was not their intention to stigmatize me.
In fact, they themselves were victims and did not know any better.
Thus, I love them and am free to achieve my goals of perfection.*

4
LIBERATION

Negative mental charges have the devastating power to disrupt one's psychological and physical inner workings. If they have become a habit, it takes enormous effort to unravel them from the subtle tangles of one's life-giving energy fields.

Unpleasant memories, perturbing thoughts, toxic ideas, and yesterday's depressing utterances all surface as constant complaints, stored-up resentments, pent-up anger, self-deprecation and lovelessness – a combination of destructive ingredients that ultimately unsettle individuals who allow themselves to fall prey to them.

One cannot avoid having been born into an aggressive home, amongst hostile people, under grievous moral and socioeconomic injunctions. This reality has its roots in the past and complaining only makes it worse – it does not eliminate it.

Indulging in deplorable memories becomes a form of masochism that strengthens what one cannot eliminate, even though there are means for overcoming and forgetting them.

Every time one relies on self-pity in times of failure, one gets more comfortable with it and holds on to it out of habit. Thus, to turn things around, the decision to be happy is urgent.

✳

Reincarnation has brought you into a home that you consider inadequate for your progress, causing you to suffer. Perhaps you yourself chose it some time ago in order to adapt to the reparative process.

Everyone is linked to the individuals they need in order to evolve. Even so, remaining imprisoned by such tormenting circumstances is an accommodating attitude toward the negative and the perturbing, whereas there are invaluable means for liberation.

Problems arise in order to be solved.

Difficulties are tests that challenge the value of one's knowledge and one's ability to persevere.

If you would rather feel sorry for yourself, no one can help you.

Resentment, fear and complaints about the past will make you even more dependent on the circumstances, in which you unconsciously find support so that you do not have to struggle for the restoration of peace and the attainment of joy.

You cannot and must not incorporate into your life the harmful predictions, the vulgar or depressing utterances that others have directed at you, or the verbal, moral and physical aggressions of which you have been a victim. That is all in the past and done. Nevertheless, diverting their harmful effects is a task you must fulfill.

You know you are not what they have accused you of. But if due to your psychological fragility you have assimilated their imprecations into your personality and believed them, break the shackles and exercise your freedom.

You are a rough stone in need of polishing. Even though you may be rough on the outside, you have the brightness of the stars on the inside, and it is up to you to release it.

Start this new process in your life right now.

Give yourself the chance to prove to yourself how much you have and you will succeed.

Experience the pleasure of rebuilding your future and you will start being happy right away.

Divine Assistance permeates my being and encourages me all the days of my life.

I endeavor to abandon habituations and discouragement, invigorating myself with prayer and working to attain higher resources.

The shadows that envelop me linger because I sustain them with my thoughts.

I will excel at personal effort and, showered by Divine Light,

I will restore myself and be happy.

5
HEALTH AND WELL-BEING

The planning of any project determines the quality of its future completion. Forecasts and details, calculations and references, organizational charts and execution all form the working basis that leads to success or failure.

From planning to completion, any changes must be studied first so that they may be introduced without harming the overall endeavor or causing excessive, unforeseen expenses.

Along the same lines, a meticulous sowing of thistles, followed by frequent fertilization, will result in no other crop but thistles.

People become what they think, what they nourish mentally and work on until it becomes ingrained.

Unfortunately, most people cherish only negative ideas, pessimism and malaise. As a result, they weaken their moral resistance, debilitate their spiritual qualities and feed off of their own delusions.

There are some trials that are inevitable because they proceed from excesses in previous lifetimes. Nevertheless, through uplifting mental and humane constructions, they may be changed, mitigated and even released, because healthy acts garner merit for overcoming harmful ones.

Do not hold on to your noxious atavisms by reliving them, commenting on them, or reconstructing them in your mental and verbal fields. They will never go away as long as you do not let them.

You complain of failures, disappointments, infirmities, lovelessness; however, you hold fast to them such that you lose your sense of evaluating reality. You label yourself as unhappy, get stuck there, and make no effort to change.

Conventional wisdom rightly states: *A rolling stone gathers no moss,* suggesting a change in course, movement, achievement.

Strive to disregard unpleasant, upsetting occurrences.

Plan your present, set goals for the future, and get to work without moping, without self-pity, without bitterness.

You can and must change your environment for the better.

It is not enough simply to ask God to help you. You have to do your part; otherwise you will achieve very little or nothing at all. Health or illness, well-being or unwellness – it all depends on you.

There is a story about a sage who was walking with his disciples on a winding pathway, when they came upon a godly man on his knees praying to God to help him pull his cart out of the quagmire.

Everyone felt sorry for the devotee, but continued on their way.

After they had gone a few more miles, they came upon another man whose cart had also gotten stuck in a quagmire. This one was complaining angrily, but was actually trying as hard as he could to free the cart.

Moved, the sage asked his disciples to help the man. They all worked together and pulled the cart out right away. The traveler thanked them and continued happily on his way.

The surprised disciples asked their master: "The first man was praying and was pious, yet we didn't help him. The second was rebellious and was even swearing, yet he received our help. How come?"

The noble teacher explained calmly:

"The one who was praying was waiting for God to come and do the job that he himself should have done. The other, though desperate out of ignorance, was actually doing something; thus he deserved assistance."

Therefore, the ideal would be not to complain at all but to think correctly in order to pull the cart of your existence out of the quagmire and proceed happily on your way with health and well-being.

Divine Love floods me with peace.

Its presence leads me to my neighbor, whom I begin to love.

I find myself lacking toward God and my neighbor.

But finally, I love and renew myself; I am fulfilled, rejoicing

in love, which is the essential goal of life.

6
LOVE ABOVE ALL THINGS

Jesus recommended that love be the cornerstone of every undertaking. He regarded it as the greatest commandment and summed up the whole *Law and all the Prophets as love for God above all things and one's neighbor as oneself.*

All human achievements, ambitions and goals are present in this threefold guideline.

Love for God means to respect and preserve life in all its expressions, making oneself an integral part of Him, conscious of the cosmic whole.

Responsibility toward nature – not attacking or devaluing it, but contributing to its development and harmony – expresses the love that contributes to the Divine Work, honoring its Author.

Love for one's neighbor is a consequence of the love dedicated to the Genitor. It demonstrates the fraternity that should unite everyone as His beloved children making their way back to Him.

Without this sentiment toward one's neighbor, one feels bewildered in loneliness and becomes weak, losing heart during illuminating activities.

Love for oneself, without egomaniacal passion, will lift one to the heights of plenitude, helping one to develop the unknown treasures that lie dormant within.

This love manifests as a way to preserve and dignify one's physical existence, harmonizing it with the whole, becoming a center that radiates a joy, peace and well-being that permeates all.

✳

See if you are abiding by the Master's recommendation. In that perfect synthesis you will satisfy all the needs for your current existence and you will find the solution to all your problems.

Calmly assess your behavior toward God, your neighbor and yourself.

If you find you are lacking in one of the postulates of the great triad, set about to correct the deficiency and change your conduct to reflect your coming to plenitude.

You will certainly discover the necessity of loving the Heavenly Father and your neighbor as best you can. However, you have restrictions or passions concerning yourself.

At times you detest yourself, whereas at other times you make excuses, stating that you are a victim of others.

You must love yourself rightly.

✳

Apply yourself to wholesome reflection regarding your deficiencies, in order to correct them, and your good qualities, in order to enhance them. Use strictness without harshness and love without sentimentality to set out on the pathway of balance and growth.

Loving yourself means perfecting yourself spiritually, emotionally and physically. With no contempt for any component of the harmonious whole that you are, love yourself and strive tenaciously to overcome your deficiencies each and every day by setting new guidelines and promising targets. You will reach them by being generous, active and persevering in the good, in relation to yourself.

Divine Power endows me with all I need for a happy life.

What I lack is certainly not important; I have no real need for it.

Unlike people incarcerated in dissatisfaction, owners of hard-earned but useless things, I have the means of discernment for achieving health and peace.

True possession will never be taken from me. True possession I shall attain.

7
POSSESSIONS

True possessors are always the best givers. Whatever one possesses, one owes. In offering something, one actually possesses it. In life's accounting, true ownership means the good spread around to provide joy; it is not something to be stored away, a useless resource.

The true gift enriches the giver as well as the recipient. Conventionally, those who scrimp and save will become wealthy. Almost always, however, they grow stingy by falling in love with their assets, thus becoming their prisoner.

Consequently, there are systems that teach how to save, generating investments that produce profits and opportunities.

Those who become *rich* this way live in constant anxiety due to fluctuations in the exchange rate, the stock exchange and securities. They are poor in the higher sentiments and are victims of financial greed.

Wealth per se is neither good nor bad; it depends on who uses it and how it is used.

Wealth easily generates attachment and the fear of losing it; it impoverishes others as it sleeps in the coffers of usury, allowing poverty to become widespread.

✳

Learn to share in order to partake better.

Whatever you own will eventually change hands, but what you are will remain, unconsumed.

Ponder the transience of physical existence and you will understand the urgent need to make use of it properly.

The unstoppable march of time demonstrates the fragility of things before its relentlessness in relation to all that is of the earth.

Only intellectual and moral achievements have the flavor of eternity.

Therefore, amass spiritual acquisitions that will broaden your horizons of understanding, of life, presenting you with a better picture of the meaning and purpose of corporeal existence.

With a correct vision as to how you should proceed, you will be freeing yourself of countless degenerative factors that have taken hold in your personality, and which are responsible for the problems, illnesses and dissatisfactions that afflict you.

You will no longer fight over trifles, nor will aggressions affect you, for they are of no importance. Your aspirations will be higher.

You will not feel more important or less important according to the game of deceitful references, of the useless competitions on the earthly stage. Your achievements will not be measured by cheers or jeers.

You will live in peace and will have all you need, without the unnecessary torment of the superfluous.

✳

Life gives you everything, provided you put forth the effort to get it. But it also takes everything away, for no one can hold on to assets that do not belong to them.

May health, peace, joy, work and self-actualization be the rare coins that you need for the human journey. They will open the doors to the future for you on the pathway of immortality – your ultimate and only goal.

The Divine Stimulus urges me to advance.

*The laws of incessant change are at
work everywhere, teaching me about renewal
and progress.*

*I am driven by a higher Power that propels me
to the summits of life.*

*The valley is dark and the mountain
conquered is light.*

*Happy, healthy and whole, I am motivated to
succeed and grow.*

8
DISSATISFACTION AND UTOPIAS

Dissatisfaction is responsible for many of the ills and sufferings in the social fabric, creating imbalances that could easily be avoided.

By using mechanisms of evasion, individuals avoid assuming their own reality. They create models of fictitious happiness, to which they shift their aspirations, producing and clinging to states of nonconformity and discontentment, wasting excellent opportunities for self-knowledge and fulfillment.

These standards become their goals, although they are unlikely to reach them. In the event that they actually do reach them, they remain stuck in the same state of morbidity and maladjustment because such goals are fallacious.

Minutia become essential, and details that differ from what they consider to be beautiful, healthy, aesthetic and happy become highly important, thus keeping them stuck in misery.

Rebellious in character and perturbing in behavior, they belittle the invaluable resources available to them and they long only for what they would like to be, have, and appear to be.

In this climate of discontent, they wait for a miracle that will never occur from the outside in. They do not put forth the effort to transform their outlook and change their attitude from the inside out.

✳

Immerse yourself in self-knowledge and rediscover yourself.

You are according to what you have made of yourself in the course of time.

Your matrices lie in the spiritual past, which you can no longer reach. However, by means of new behaviors, you can change the pace and occurrences of life.

Examine yourself and have the courage to face your situation, developing paradigms and realistic goals that you might actually reach.

Running from yourself will not take you anywhere, for you can never disassociate yourself from your reality.

Start a program of self-worth, analyzing facts and events, according to whether or not they deserve consideration.

Do not blame anyone or anything for what you consider to be your failures.

When irresponsible individuals make no effort to change what can be changed, they shift the responsibility to what they see as bad circumstances, to other people, or they blame themselves, preferring complaint and commiseration to fruitful effort. Time, place, society, government, envy of others, unhealthy competition, bad luck or weakness are the *ingredients* for justifying habituation, the false suffering of which they believe themselves the object.

Reach for the stars.

Impose new concepts on life and strive to experience them in a spiritually constructive way.

Those who feel sorry for themselves refuse to receive help from their neighbor.

Dissatisfied individuals, besides being ungrateful, are rebellious and lazy; they prefer the *darkness* of complaining and procrastinating rather than the *light* of liberating progress.

Do not allow yourself existential utopias; depart on the conquest of true accomplishments.

Divine Consciousness showers me with peace.

My misconceptions are clarified and I am at peace as I ponder the countless options for inner harmony within my reach.

Before me lies the present, preparing the future. The past entails the lessons learned, and the advantages of that knowledge provide me with support for inner growth.

I trust and renew myself, at peace in the good.

9
BEFORE ONE'S CONSCIENCE

Among all the inner scourges that torment humans, producing unnamable afflictions, the guilty conscience stands out.

It insidiously takes root and, like an acid, it corrodes the gears of the emotions, fostering the eruption of maddening inner conflicts.

Arising from psychological insecurity in judging one's own actions, a guilty conscience opens an abyss between what has been done and what should not have been done, cruelly flogging those who suffer its dogged persecution.

Due to their own weakness, individuals allow themselves incorrect behaviors that appeal to their sensations, but as soon as these cease, they surrender to self-punitive regret, trying to correct their foolishness, and being immediately assailed by a guilty conscience.

Perversely, it punishes the offender inwardly, but it does not alter the course of the action's consequences, nor does it make things right with the injured party. On the contrary, despite being an unforgiving creditor, it unconsciously arouses new desires, repeated behaviors, and ever-increasing punishment...

Self-punishment is an atavism of hypocritical religious, moral and social behaviors, which do not hesitate to make the wrong recommendation; thus, it must be eliminated thoroughly and immediately.

✳

You cannot prevent or avoid what you have already done.

Once the arrow is released, it follows its trajectory.

Therefore, determine the effects and rectify them when negative.

If your action was reproachable, take measures to correct it as soon you can.

If your attitude was the result of a personal conflict that does not correspond to what you believe or who you are, practice balance and stay vigilant.

Weak are all who consider themselves weak but do not put forth the effort to become strong.

If you *excuse* your mistake with self-punishment in order to appease the guilt, you will soon make it again.

Look at life as it is and your circumstances as they are.

Eradicate from your mind all ideas that you consider inappropriate, harmful or dysfunctional. Make a real effort to replace them with others that are healthy, balanced and dignified. When you do not have a collection of lofty thoughts to ponder, you are overcome by thoughts of a venal, childish, pernicious nature, which become familiar and drive you to act accordingly.

Every achievement starts in the mind. Designed on the mental plane, it materializes at the first opportunity.

Therefore, think correctly, letting go of any unhealthy ideas that will create a guilty conscience.

Whenever you err, start over with the enthusiasm you had at the start. Dignity, harmony, and balance between conscience and conduct come at a price: perseverance in your duty. If, however, you have difficulty in acting correctly due to a deeply rooted attitude, turn to prayer with sincerity, and Divine Consciousness will uplift you to peace.

Divine Truth penetrates and transforms me.

As I allow myself to be imbued with it, |
I am renewed, and none of the accusations
leveled at me by frivolous and
bad individuals touch or disturb me.

I allow myself to follow the path of liberation
with enthusiasm and peace.

Divine Truth floods my conscience. I think and
act correctly.

10
THE LIBERATING TRUTH

The world is clear full of *truths*. Weak concepts, bizarre philosophies, preposterous ideas, thoughts without logical structure – all are presented as truths and eagerly received.

Alongside these and others that are even stranger and more incoherent swarm people's own individual *truths* in warlike struggles of factions, classes and currents that wish to dominate.

The truth, however, reigns supreme, imperturbable, over the degrading passions, waiting to disclose itself to those who aspire to high-mindedness and who embrace aesthesia, knowledge and reason, immersing themselves in its enlightening content.

Anything that afflicts, impassions and fetters does not even have the semblance of the truth, for such things only serve to torment individuals, driving them to paroxysms and delusions.

The truth liberates, soothes and consoles.

The union of individuals with its contents unfolds in an atmosphere of surrender and peace. It progresses slowly, surely and thoughtfully, producing the inner transformation of those who set out to acquire it.

✳

Whatever you resolve, without analyzing it deeply, will become truth to you.

Believing it to be true, you will see it as real.

You need to submit your beliefs to the test of reason to see which ones can endure the scalpel of logic and common sense.

Therefore, any criticisms and reproaches leveled at you ought not disrupt you and throw you off balance.

First of all, draw up your action plan and make up your mind to carry it out. Shielding yourself with the ideal you have espoused, press on.

Do not argue over your plans and aspirations with the world's *owners of the truth*, especially those who are particularly close to you, because those individuals are unwilling to understand you, let alone help you.

The majority of them are passionate combatants for their own transitory *truths,* which they do not give up because they are belligerent. Consequently, they become severe criticizers, aggressive sentinels and forceful fighters against others.

Pay them no mind. If you disregard their senseless opinions against you, their slanderous references and acidic comments, none of it can touch you.

But if you do heed them, they will become *truths* that trouble you and disrupt your progress, although you have a destiny to reach.

The truth gives balance; it stimulates order and respect for the ideas of others.

Fulfill your commitments, unconcerned with what others think about you, your actions, your life. You are free to act, but remember you are a slave to what you do, reaping as you have sown. The rest is unimportant, unless you decide to make it important.

The truth always satisfies. So, let its power pervade you, and carry on tranquilly, supported by it.

Divine Forgiveness sweetens and soothes me. It gives me the extent of Love's therapeutic power. I begin to see the world and people differently, correctly, positively.

I overcome the resentments that used to torment me.

I begin to live without the chains that used to hold me back.

I recover the joy of living and being natural, loving all with tenderness, even those who do not correspond to my affection.

All is well with me now because I feel good about life.

11
THE TRAGEDY OF RESENTMENT

Psychosocial, socio-emotional, economic and other pressures trigger various disorders that affect a wide range of society.

Causing fear, anxiety and resentment, they destabilize the nervous system and cause serious neuroses, which are nearly always somatized and are responsible for allergic, gastrointestinal, metabolic infirmities in general, fostering degenerative processes.

Under pressure, fragile temperaments look for escape mechanisms and either fall into phobic and depressive states, or resort to aggressiveness to affirm and defend their personality.

A lot of psychological residue takes root in their emotional and mental field, leading to behavioral disturbances and various diseases that cannot be diagnosed accurately.

Sensitive individuals who cannot endure and overcome such constricting pressures lapse into resentment, which makes them miserable and predisposes them to react all the time by shooting poisonous darts at their real or imagined enemies.

Some poison themselves with bitterness and wither away. Others subconsciously become victims of emotional, financial and social setbacks. Many have no self-esteem, see themselves as worthless, and play the game of self-destruction.

Resentment is responsible for many of the tragedies that take place every day.

*

Resentment is a poison that kills its host. As it vibrates in the emotions, it wreaks havoc on the more subtle nerve equipment and produces dysrhythmia, oscillating blood pressure and heart problems.

It is not worth letting oneself be poisoned by resentment.

Resentment does not always manifest patently; it camouflages itself in mental fixations and sometimes goes completely unnoticed.

There are resentful people who do not even realize it.

A serious self-examination will help you identify it in the folds of your soul. Then, as you continue your quest and analysis, you will uncover its roots, when it first began, and why it became ingrained in your being and began disturbing you.

You will be surprised to discover that you are responsible for giving it shelter and strength, letting yourself be consumed by it.

People who have been mean to you – family, acquaintances, teachers – in childhood and throughout your life, have no idea to this day of what they did and/or still do to you. They remain oblivious to their excesses and inconsistencies in that regard. They, themselves, suffered the same attacks when they were children, and are only reacting as others did toward them.

Your first step is to sympathize with them and realize they are neither responsible for, nor aware of, their actions, nor are they ill-intentioned toward you. Consequently, you can understand and forgive them, setting yourself free.

Removing the unjust cause of resentment, you will immediately awaken in a landscape without darkness. You will rediscover life and disarm yourself in relation to others whom you have disliked, or with whom you have remained on your guard.

Moreover, the harm they do to you can upset you only with your consent. Otherwise, it will return to its source.

Therefore, live without bitterness.

Purify yourself. Resentment – never!

Divine Consciousness opens me up to the infinite and astounds me.

I leave my suffocating and agonizing limitations behind and enter the grandeur of life, in which I am expanding.

Immersed in my inner world, I see, hear and perceive reality without barriers, without fog – a reality from which I have come and to which I will return.
I am one with my Father and am free.

12
EXTRA-PHYSICAL PERCEPTION

There is an urgent need to have an inner life in order to achieve identification with reality.

The world of the physical senses, in view of its significance and purpose of putting individuals in contact with external manifestations, distances them from profound yet subtle insights into a full life.

Restricting individuals to the realm of objective manifestations, it keeps them from broadening their paranormal capabilities, which open the *portals* to the infinite field of causality.

Immersed in an ocean of vibrations, energy and mind, and surrounded by waves and incessant thoughts, individuals should widen their psychic capacity to be inundated with extra-physical content, which does affect them, even when they are unaware of it.

People are endowed with transceiver antennas that render them unwitting instruments of complex forces that drive them to surprising attitudes, which they could change to express their preferences, rather than being docile instruments without a will of their own.

Within this vast range of para-physical occurrences, telepathy, intuition, clairvoyance, clairaudience, inspiration, precognition and retro-cognition bestow indisputable blessings that are within reach of whosoever seeks them with a moral and conscientious attitude.

✳

You are an instrument of constant psychic exchange, even though you may not realize it.

You are continuously emitting and receiving vibrations, ideas and mental energies. However you direct your thought, you will attune yourself to other thoughts of the same quality, producing affinity.

You live in the vibratory world you choose due to your psychic and emotional preferences, repelling and attracting corresponding waves. According to the pattern you have cultivated, you are surrounded by identical psychic responses.

Bearing in mind the indestructibility of the soul, there are discarnate spirits within that colossal range of reality, and you interact with them, even though you may not always perceive them.

By educating yourself inwardly, you can learn to receive their thoughts and maintain productive communication with them, which will begin to prepare you for the future, when you rid yourself of the material envelope.

Without your knowing it, they influence your life, either helping you when they are good, or perturbing you when bad.

Because they are the souls of men and women who used to live on the earth, they have held on to their values , sometimes suffering and causing suffering for a long time, out of ignorance or perversity, habituation or envy.

If you work on your inner silence and morals, you will attune yourself to the High-Order Spirits who guide you and want to share their wisdom and love with you, making your upward progress easier.

Consequently, you will enter regions of imperishable light, experiencing blissful, transcendent emotions.

By developing para-physical perception, you will cease to be a confined prisoner, and you will glide through realms of ardent life, aware of the resources that God has granted you for your wholeness as an eternal individual.

The Divine Source of energy is reached through prayer.

I enter its core while I pray, and I am reinvigorated by the forces that invade me.

The higher energies restore my balance, and my vital field is recomposed, sustaining my being.

I pray and lift myself to God, thus hovering, though briefly, above human misery.

13

THE RESOURCE OF PRAYER

Prayer is the most accessible, magnificent resource there is for enabling individuals to communicate with the Creator.

An invisible bridge of subtle energies, it promotes the union of the soul with the Divine Genitor, from whom it draws forces and inspiration for the difficult commitments of existence.

Prayer does not change the battlefield, nor does it prevent the trials that foster evolution. However, it does provide endurance for the struggle and is ever encouraging and vitalizing.

It strengthens the enthusiasm of those who use it and broadens their view of reality.

It modifies their understanding and the way they tackle events, producing attunement to the Divine Thought, which governs everything.

Those who pray overcome tensions and are filled with peace.

Prayer creates the conditions and circumstances for meditation, which projects the psyche toward the higher spheres, thus balancing one's health and aspirations for a better grasp of the meaning of the physical existence and one's reincarnation.

Prayer prepares the saint, sustains the hero, inspires the researcher, and maintains life, while projecting light onto dark, threatening landscapes.

＊

No matter how whole you may feel, do not get out of the habit of prayer, so that you may remain balanced.

When you go through difficulties or face harsh trials and expiations, resort to prayer and you will notice the benefits that accrue.

Prayer is the most effective, long-lasting readily available device for maintaining your enthusiasm and preserving your ideal. It will not only preserve your moral and spiritual forces, but will also attract the good spirits, who act as God's instruments for solving many human problems.

Be constant in prayer, using its invaluable action, which will maintain you mentally in an unchanging, lofty climate.

Those who pray become renewed and enlightened, for it kindles an inner light that shines outward through special vibrations.

When you actually experience the well-being and joy that derive from prayer, you will use it more frequently and make it your language of communication with the Ardent Life.

Enveloped in its radiations, you will dilute every ill that comes near, aiding the bad people that come your way.

You will derive such comfort from prayer that it will be your constant companion, making your very existence a state of prayer.

✳

Resort to prayer at every moment of your life. In sickness and in health, in joy and in sorrow, in wealth and in poverty, in success and in failure, pray and trust in the Divine answer.

By praying, you will draw near the higher realms, and in the energy of prayer you will receive all you need to press on to victory.

Individuals seek God through prayer, and God responds through intuition about what to do and how to do it, and in so doing, they are happy.

Divine Light envelops me and scatters the outer darkness that used to besiege me with bitterness.

I let myself be enlightened, and all my problems disappear, enabling me to better see the plan for my physical existence.

Pessimism vanishes; irritation is gone.

I am destined for success, and I pursue it with a mind enriched with enthusiasm.

I am bathed in outer light; I am inner light.

14
DAYS OF DARKNESS

Coincidentally, there are days that are characterized by a string of unpleasant occurrences. Nothing seems to go right. All activities are mixed up and facts are depressing and disturbing. With each new attempt, other failures ensue, as if the order of natural events were totally upset.

On these occasions, problems pile up and pessimism settles in the mind and emotions, leading to negative memories with grim omens.

Those who suffer such injunctions tend to get discouraged and take refuge in psychological patterns of self-affliction, unhappiness, and self-contempt.

They feel besieged by colossal forces that cannot be fought against, and thus let themselves be dragged along by the contrary currents, poisoning themselves with ill humor.

These are days of trial, and not for discouragement; of challenge, and not for the cessation of effort.

The harsher the difficulties, the more should be the investment of energies and the more careful the application of moral values in the battle.

Giving up without a fight, the quicker the failure, and when one goes into battle with ideas of losing, part of the endeavor is already lost.

✳

On such dark days, which do happen periodically and, at times, become continuous, be more vigilant and thoughtful.

It is normal for there to be one or more failures when several activities are involved. Even so, an unending string of failures may have roots in pernicious spirit-related causes, where certain personages are interested in harming you, making mental and emotional space for obsessive[2] interaction.

The more you become irritable and depressed, the more you will feel fenced in, and then even more unfortunate occurrences will take shape.

Do not struggle, swimming against the current until you are exhausted. Overcome its flow by diverting the direction of the water.

There are perverse spirit minds around you interested in your failure.

Fight against their wiles with prayer, optimistic thoughts and unreserved trust in God.

Break the *succession* of mistakes by changing your mental landscape so that you do not empower the perturbing agent.

Listen to enriching music that leads you to recall pleasant memories or to make exciting plans.

Read an uplifting passage from the Gospel or other edifying work in order to renew yourself emotionally.

Get away from the hustle and bustle and get some rest; contemplate a region that will lift you out of your dismal state.

---

2 "Domination that certain spirits may acquire over certain individuals." See more on Obsession in *The Mediums' Book*, by Allan Kardec, Ch. XXIII, #237 et seq. – Tr.

Think about the blissful future that awaits you. Lift yourself to God through fervent prayer and you will break the chains of affliction.

The sun is always shining behind the gloomy clouds, and when it is placed in your inner world, no threat of darkness can begin to diminish the intensity of its light. Follow that light and, confidently and peacefully, defeat your day of failures.

Divine Energy gives rise to life everywhere and reigns supreme over me.

Undefinable, living and thinking, feeling and loving reach their climax in the human being.

This powerful energy enables me to receive new resources for growth and self-actualization.

I choose happiness. I will not give in to apathy, to the perturbing injunctions to which I have gotten used to. I am life unfolding.

I get back on my feet and acquire new patterns of thought and action to make myself whole.

15
LIFE RENEWED

L ife is the most extraordinary gift there is. It manifests
in many, many forms, obeying rhythmic cycles with
established objectives.

It cannot be avoided or even delayed on its rhythmically
fatalistic course to perfection.

Life renews itself endlessly and this phenomenon is part
of its process. Whatever is not renewed *dies*, is transformed,
upsets the dynamics of life.

Human life, in particular, is a supreme gift that must
be preserved and used effectively, expanding it to the utmost
in order to reap its benefits.

A Divine Emanation, life is the presence of the supreme
consciousness manifesting everywhere.

Inhaling and being inundated with that vital energy
is an act of intelligence, used for preserving and expanding
achievements.

In this ceaseless flow of energy, individuals' innate
possibilities blossom and they perceive the glory and joy
of living.

*

For life to pulsate abundantly within you, make a careful assessment of how you feel about yourself, how you are doing, and what you have achieved.

Have the courage to make a conscious, responsible, enriching self-analysis so that when negative results turn up, you can cope by changing your beliefs, thoughts, habits and behaviors – anything that obstructs your development, your appreciation of life and its bounty.

Old ingrained habits, negative thoughts, a weakened will, pernicious atavisms, and unreleased resentments will conspire against your plans for renewal.

You will see the need for change, but all the fixations of your existence will rise up against you, imposing restrictions, postponements, disincentives...

Among the many negative factors that will try to keep you in a state of suffering or paralysis, there is the fear of what *others* will say, of how *others* will see you, of what will befall you ... Other disturbing dynamics will emerge from your unconscious to keep you stuck at your present level.

You will believe you are too tired, old, young, weak-willed, lacking in moral strength, and unable to cope with new situations. You will give in to the temptation to remain where you are: with problems, anxieties, dissatisfaction, failures...

Even so, begin by revising your old beliefs, those that were imposed on you by persons who, though well-meaning, were ill-equipped to educate you with their derogatory opinions, their servile concepts, their dire predictions.

You are capable of overcoming pessimism and the lack of self-esteem that was foisted on you and which you eagerly accepted. This is your moment; not later or maybe never.

Change your thoughts and reasoning, directing them at success, in what you should believe and, committing yourself, you will succeed.

Then, get to work on your renewal.

✳

Old habits create strong resistance and they will fight against your desire to change.

This is a new plan, which you will go about step by step until you get good results.

Never stop renewing yourself for the better, because life does not return with the same conditions, circumstances and time, although it never ceases to manifest itself and offer opportunities.

Divine Serenity comes over me after I have fulfilled my duties.

I understand my responsibilities in life and I detach myself from conflicts.

Clear-minded, I advance step by step to acquire consciousness, and I harmonize myself, merging with the whole of the Work of God.

Serene and confident, no evil can touch me.

16
SERENITY

Serenity is the cornerstone of the moral and spiritual constructs of the human being. Without serenity, accomplishments become very difficult. It results from right conduct and an equitable consciousness, both of which provide a realistic view of events and foster the identification of the goals in life worthy of the valuable investments of bodily existence.

In the frantic pursuit of pleasure, cultural treasures are wasted and are made servants of the lower, perturbing passions, with negative consequences. The more one enjoys pleasure, the greater the need to experience even more of it in order to renew the sensations that masquerade as emotions.

Serenity is the state of concurrence between duty and right, which harmonize for the individual's benefit.

With a serene conscience, one can face every situation with poise and never fall apart emotionally. Occurrences, people and existential phenomena are seen on their true levels of importance and do not become a cause of distress, no matter how bad they may seem.

Serene individuals are content because they have overcome attachments and detachments, illusions and desires, maintaining harmony in any situation. Balanced, they are not victims of extremes; they choose the *middle path* with firm, unwavering determination.

✳

Serenity is not outward quietness or indifference, but wholeness of action devoid of anxiety or fear, insecurity or haste.

In the heat of every battle, in the eloquent lesson of the Beatitudes, or even while being crucified, Jesus maintained His serenity – although differently each time – undeterred and self-assured with unreserved trust in God.

Meditating in Varanasi, where he presented his *Four Noble Truths*, or while being hounded by terrible persecutions by the Brahmins, his fiery enemies, Buddha remained calm, totally surrendered to peace.

Preaching that intermediaries between God and humans are unnecessary, or even while being burned at the stake, Jan Huss remained faithful and serene, knowing that no one could actually end his life.

The martyrs experienced the serenity of their ideal wherever they struggled, and thus were not affected by evil or persecution by the wicked.

Serenity also comes from certainty and confidence in what one knows, does and is. It is a sure anchor rooted in the seafloor securing the ship of existence, giving it time to be prepared to sail forward.

✳

Always act with a clear conscience so that you do not fall into conflict and lose your serenity.

Love and study yourself, choosing what is best and long-lasting for your days, and you will never retreat. However, if you do err, if you do compromise yourself, if you do become regretful, do not feel afflicted with guilt. Recompose yourself, correct the mistake, recover and recapture your serenity. Without it, you will hinder your progress by experiencing suffering that you could otherwise avoid. Serenity is life.

The Divine Reality awakens me so that
I may know myself, thus discovering and
identifying myself.

My quest is no longer clothed in illusion, but in
the certainty of my next encounter with reality.

I am what I am, on my way to being
an ideal person.

I accept and perfect myself, requiring nothing of
anyone, loving everyone, and allowing myself to
be led by Reality.

17

ENCOUNTER WITH REALITY

The deluded *ego* seeks to survive by using innumerable mechanisms to escape reality, and it expresses itself using different masks in order not to be identified.

It disguises itself in interpersonal relationships, at times demanding toward others, at other times excessively hard on itself, projecting its conflicts or introjecting its unfulfilled aspirations. Subconsciously, the ego has a misconceived idea of itself. It does not have the courage to face reality, to overcome it when negative, or to improve it when favorable.

Fixating on the illusion of conflicts, it is careful to appear conciliatory – the subconscious attitude of what it would really like to be, and with the appropriate appearance – expressing itself as a happy, fulfilled person.

Due to the breakdown of ethical values in society, the fear of revealing oneself to others generates reactions and deception, in which one seeks psychological rewards – always unfulfilling. Because the ego's *foundations* are shaky, the *constructs* of apparent well-being soon crumble, and the individual lapses into repressed anxieties and aggressions due to emotional transference for inner compensation.

There is a whole range of human attitudes that are far from being authentic and which result from postures that are opposite to their reality.

Notwithstanding a few exceptions involving non-passionate or non-extreme idealists, most people who protest against something, whatever it might be, hide subconscious desires, which they repress due to a lack of moral value to express them appropriately.

Puritanical individuals, who keep an eye on other people's *misconduct*, project the very inner state that they seek to combat in others, because they are unwilling to combat it in themselves.

Biting, persistent critics, with a *clinical eye* on other people's errors and miseries, harbor personal insecurity. They have great contempt for themselves and make up for it by being aggressive.

Those who usually identify themselves with pain and affliction, an exaggerated and therefore inauthentic humility, unconsciously externalize a paranoid state alongside an unquenchable desire to seek attention.

Those who always rationalize every occurrence, finding justifications for their own failures and mistakes, actually fear themselves and have no emotional structure for breaking free of conflicts.

Without aggression, sentimentality, or anxiety about unjustifiable confessions, reveal yourself to your friends so that they can relax and reveal themselves to you as they are.

Do not be a critic of other people's lives, disrupting their *games* with the presentation of your truths. If you strip them of their support, do you have anything to offer them in terms of behavior and security?

So, watch yourself and relax. Let yourself be identified by your great strengths and weaknesses, allowing those close to you the same disclosure and trust.

Only with those we know well, can we feel really at ease.

Divine Vitality sweeps over me and I absorb
it in an excellent emotional disposition.

I am free of the toxic burdens of psychological
burnout: sorrow, hatred, jealousy, revenge, envy,
bitterness.

I am of healthy provenance. Illness is an
accident along the way, but it does not prevent
me from progressing.

Healthy and confident, I advance, vitalized by
the breath of the Generating Fount of Life.

18

THE BLESSING OF HEALTH

Health is the result of several factors that come together for psychophysical harmony. Coming from the spirit, energy produces cells and sustains them during the ministry of physical life, thus enabling them to fulfill their purpose.

Radiating by means of the perispirit, energy fosters the preservation of the body, providing resistance against the constant aggression of destructive agents.

When this energy becomes disrupted, these microbial invaders win the battle and settle in, giving rise to illnesses.

In the area of emotional and mental phenomena, due to the delicate workings of the apparatus through which they are expressed, the incidence of the spirit's energy wave in these subtle *tissues* is the cause of imbalance, rendering disorders and alienating afflictions more serious.

In this state of affairs, undermined by pernicious mental discharges and the disorder they cause, individuals' deep structures foster attunement with disruptive and vengeful spirits, who gain access to the mental field, producing obsessions.

The preservation of one's health requires constant preventive care and ongoing therapeutics for the valuable achievements for which one is destined during reincarnation.

✴

Given the myriad of pathologies that afflict humans, maintaining one's mental and emotional stability is crucial for staying healthy.

Thus, always see yourself as healthy and cultivate optimistic thoughts based on love, ennobling action and hope.

Maintain your inner peace by ridding yourself of mental debris, because it may poison you and act as a stimulus for disruptive microbes.

If infirmity does pay you a visit, take advantage of it for invaluable insights into your behavior, and reprogram your activities.

Think about health and earnestly desire it, without imposition or pressure, but with noble intent.

Plan to be healthy and useful, foreseeing yourself as healed and hardworking in your family and social life, and as a valuable instrument of your community.

Connect with the Generous Source from which all forces emanate, and absorb the resources you need for rebalancing yourself.

Replenish your mind with thoughts of peace, compassion, solidarity, forgiveness and tenderness, involving yourself emotionally with Life so that you feel you are part of it, conscious and happy.

In any circumstance, illness is a blessed trial, except when, deforming, alienating or limiting, it constitutes a timely expiation that the Sovereign Laws utilize in order to help the evolution of the unrighteous, who almost all of us are in one way or another.

If you are healthy, use the opportunity to preserve yourself, increasing and improving your production.

If you are sick, thank God and expand your mental horizons in love so that you may recuperate today or later, moving forward in peace and confidence.

*Divine Understanding hovers over
and pervades me. It mellows me out and calms
me down.*

*I perceive the world and other individuals in a
positive and fraternal manner.*

*I become more creative and healthy, relating
well with my neighbor.*

*My understanding is expanded and I live in
peace with myself and others.*

19
UNDERSTANDING

Understanding is the ability that best contributes to success in human relationships, because it validates the other person's positive and negative qualities. It reflects great spiritual development, through which it offers support and guidance to the one who seeks it in difficult situations.

Understanding distends solidarity, providing the necessary therapeutic resources according to the needs of the moment. Without agreeing with everything that is said, or rejecting it outright, understanding benefits the listener, who is then truly heard.

Humans are instinctively gregarious and need to be with one another in healthy interaction in order to receive and provide stimuli that lead to their development.

Due to numerous factors, human understanding regarding other people's limitations and problems has become scarcer, something necessary, yet rare.

Imperiously eager to communicate, individuals look for relationships and yearn to disclose themselves to each other. Yet, the human heart dreads being exposed. What they are is their troubling treasure and they are afraid to see it despised. Their actual way of being is different from the image they portray and fear losing. This is so because they do not expect to receive understanding.

✳

The world is full of *deaf* people talking with one another; of *mute* socialization being expressed in intense, *silent* interactions.

There is much talk about *nothing,* resolving a broad spectrum of problems that remain...

When people approach you to talk, try to listen and register their words. Perhaps you cannot offer the best advice, or do what is expected of you, but quite often they only want a *listening ear.*

Give them your attention and you will encourage them, making them feel worthy of interest.

If they decide to trust you and open up, respect their problems and help them if you can.

On your part, overcome the fear of opening up. Of course you cannot neglect prudence or balance, but it is healthy to dialog and unveil the panels hidden by the *ego* or masked to reflect unrealistic images.

As a frail human being, living honestly with others will contribute effectively to your inner harmony.

So, be empathetic and patient, a fraternal therapist.

Do not create stereotypes or label people with images that are but a passing phase.

We are all undergoing continuous transformations, and we are not always today what we seemed to have been yesterday. New experiences and lessons have been added to the lives of others, as is the case with you. It is the inexorable imperative of progress in action.

In understanding your neighbors and relating with them, you will be kinder to yourself; realizing their weaknesses, you will be more attentive to your own limits and will seek to grow, loving others and yourself more.

Divine Balance keeps me in harmony.
I go within to know myself. I go outside myself
to be useful.

I must be generous toward myself,
others and Life.

Divine Balance has touched me gently, like
springtime shedding dew on the rosebud, and it
has made me blossom fully.

20
PSYCHOLOGICAL MATURITY

The interpersonal relationship reveals people's behavior in relation to themselves and others. In early attempts, individuals hide their reality in the great preoccupation with appearance. But as connections narrow, people's caution gives way to emotional relaxation, and little by little the *mask* falls away.

This phenomenon results from the closeness that time provides the relationship.

The conduct of healthy, accomplished people holds no surprises because there is an interaction between their inner and outer lives – true psychological maturity. After self-awareness, which brings about self-acceptance, the outer is explored and new and enriching experiences are welcome. Balance marks the personality, and there are no eccentricities or abrupt changes, as is the case between elation and depression.

Such individuals have attained plenitude, radiating this human achievement all around.

In the alternate behavior, where joy and sorrow, trust and suspicion, love and animosity are mixed together, immaturity and a lack of self-discovery foster states of instability and misery, leading to somatic emotional disorders that surface destructively in the body.

In a relationship, such reflections generate imbalances that worsen and become disastrous, pushing their victims into obsessive-compulsive or depressive states.

✳

In your quest for growth, get a feel for the conflict between your inner and outer reality.

Do not become upset with reactive people, who are angry at themselves and *spew* their foul mood at others. Be courteous so that your bilious state does not dictate your behavior.

In your turn, do not become such a personality yourself, always reacting when you should and could act.

Your action and reaction express how you are on the inside, as well as how you really feel and see what is happening there.

Therefore, do not waste your energies putting on masks; instead, apply them to the ongoing work of self-improvement and inner growth until you exteriorize your achievements in friendliness, warmth and love.

Any attempt to change the world and make it spin as you see fit is a delusion. But if you dedicate yourself to an inner transformation that is reflected in better behavior, you will reach the true goal of psychological maturity.

With this deepening of your spiritual self, complete health will be your friend in the grand purpose that takes you in search of personal and human self-realization.

✳

Jesus never groveled before the falsely rich and powerful, nor was He ever arrogant toward the poor and the suffering. The line of balance between His inner and outer Self demonstrated His moral, spiritual and intellectual superiority, which makes Him our Model in every respect, the perfect example of a fulfilling, psychological maturity.

TIMES OF CONSCIENTIOUSNESS[3]

630. *How can we distinguish between good and evil?*
"Good is everything that is in harmony with God's law, whereas evil is everything that deviates from it. Thus, doing what is good conforms to God's law, while doing evil infringes on it."
(Kardec, Allan. *The Spirits' Book*)[4]

*T*he unmatured man was dazzled by the shimmering constellations in the heavens and decided to conquer them. But upon realizing the magnitude of the undertaking, he deemed it impossible, so he decided to conquer the earth, his kindly mother.

The battles matured him and the difficulties expanded his view of reality, enabling him to see that this, too, was impossible. Hence, he decided to conquer his beloved native land.

He pursued the risky endeavor and actually did gain social status and power; however, the number of disappointments and amount of bitterness caused him to give that up too, so he decided to merely conquer the town where he lived.

Favorable political circumstances put him in high places, but just as he was ready to reap the rewards, the artifices of hostile, belligerent groups defeated him.

Even more matured and thoughtful, he turned to his own family, and with old age approaching, he endeavored to conquer them.

---

[3] Governed by or conforming to the dictates of conscience; an active moral sense governing all one's actions and painstaking efforts to follow one's conscience. (www.merriam-webster.com) – Tr.

[4] Kardec, Allan, *The Spirits' Book*, 4th edition (International Spiritist Council, 2010). – Tr.

But conflicting interests in his home and amongst his offspring got him thrown out, for he had become a burden. He was too old in the opinion of the young, ambitious dreamers — the kind he himself had been at one time...

That is when he became fully aware of his reality, and only then did he understand the importance of conquering himself.

*

Times of conscientiousness.

The lust for pleasure dominates the masses, and anxious individuals feel unsettled and hurt one another. They rush headlong into exhaustive enjoyments but never feel satisfied.

A wave of mediocrity swells and threatens to wash away the ennobling achievements of society.

A violent breach of values promotes the fear of living an honorable life, making room for the prevalence of folly and crime.

This change in moral behavior alters the scope of discernment and rubs elbows with vileness and promiscuity.

Consequently, people hesitate to choose moral, sound conduct.

The bizarre and hostile replace the beautiful and peaceable, making it hard to tell what is real or imaginary, noble or ignoble.

There is a lack of greatness, love and selflessness on the earth these days.

The great nations are in turmoil and their citizens, overwhelmed.

Partially-developed countries are anxious, insecure.

And victimized by economic misery, developing countries experience hunger, calamitous diseases, unemployment, and widespread mania.

In all of them, however, violence, promiscuity and the decay of customs reign supreme.

Distressed individuals, however, seek other paths of affirmation.

The need for peace and a longing for well-being are inherent to human nature.

This search arises in times of conscientiousness, when one discovers genuine needs and knows how to distinguish them from nonsense, superficiality and disillusionment.

Pondering these circumstances, which are predominant in various segments of contemporary society, we decided to write this work.

We are inspired by The Spirits' Book by Allan Kardec, which is an inexhaustible source of wisdom, a much-needed repository of liberating lessons for self-discovery, self-enlightenment.

Intellectual and moral maturity fosters conscientiousness and this drives one toward the truth and life.

We have selected twenty themes and have examined them from the perspective of conscientiousness, based on the studies of the Master of Lyon. They propose a sure course for those who are willing to reflect on them.

We were not concerned about following the questions[5] in ascending order; instead, we selected the themes and gave them

---

[5] *The Spirits' Book* contains 1,019 questions proposed by Kardec and answered by the Spirits. All quotations herein are from the 4th edition, published by the International Spiritist Council. – Tr.

a special classification in order to promote broader observations about life, behavior and human experiences.

We certainly do not presume to believe that we are adding anything new to the specialists on human beings and their moral behavior.

We are pleased to offer a little of what we have on behalf of the modern-day, hard-working man and woman who are aware of the fact that, while striving to construct a happier world, their ambition should be to conquer themselves and not others.

JOANNA DE ÂNGELIS
Salvador, Brazil, September 11, 1991

1
ACQUIRING CONSCIENTIOUSNESS

At the moment of conscientiousness, that is, the point at which you begin using balance to discern right from wrong, you will have reached the high point as a human being.

A natural effect of the evolutionary process, this accomplishment will enable you to evaluate critical factors such as Good and Evil, right and wrong, responsibility and irresponsibility, honor and dishonor, the noble and the ignoble, the legal and the illegal, liberty and libertinism.

Using intangible data, you will know how to choose existential phenomena and events, making those that provide you with well-being, harmony, moral progress, and tranquility your sure guidelines.

Conscientiousness is not intellectual in nature, that is, an activity of the brain's mechanisms; rather, it is a force that drives them, because it is born in evolutionary experiences externalized as actions.

We often find it in uneducated individuals, yet absent in learned ones.

If we were to analyze the behavior of certain specialists in respiratory problems, that is, those who intellectually understand the damage caused by smoking, alcoholism and other addictive drugs, but who indulge in any of such scourges themselves, we would have to say that they have not yet acquired conscientiousness. Their knowledge is so weak that they lack the fortitude to personally promote healthy behavior.

By extension, those who commit the crime of abortion, supported by erroneous legal arguments or so-called *rights,* as well as by persons who encourage or perform it, display the same lack of conscientiousness. They are behaving according to instinct and sometimes cunning and accommodation masqueraded as intelligence.

Other individuals may lack intellectual knowledge, but they have the lucidity to face life's challenges, choosing non-aggressive and dignified behavior, even at the cost of personal sacrifice.

One's conscientiousness can be trained by practicing lofty moral values aimed at the good of others, and consequently, one's own good.

The effort to acquire healthy habits leads to awareness in relation to life's duties and responsibilities.

Heirs to themselves, to past experiences, individuals evolve in stages, acquiring new resources, correcting previous errors, and adding accomplishments. They never actually regress, even when apparently reincarnated within the *walls* of limiting diseases that block the body, mind or emotions, thus generating suffering. Evolutionary achievements may remain *dormant* for future commitments, when they will emerge lucid.

Acquiring conscientiousness is a life challenge. It deserves examination, consideration and work.

✳

Your earthly existence may be seen as a business that you should manage as competently and as carefully as possible.

You will have to work with concrete and other, more abstract data in the area of planning activities in order to succeed. All hard work and dedication will translate into gains, which you will always be able to use in difficult situations.

A few concise rules will help you with this undertaking, such as:

Manage your conflicts. Psychological conflict is inherent in human nature and everyone experiences it.

Avoid following role models. They too are vulnerable to the same injunctions that you experience, and they sometimes make mistakes, which in no way should be discouraging.

Trust more in your own abilities, honoring yourself with the effort to continue to improve without becoming discouraged. If you err, try again; if you get it right, move on.

Do not avoid facing your problems by employing erroneous, compromising, detrimental tactics. They will emerge later on as unfortunate dependencies.

Fight off depression, and work without self-pity or laziness.

Remember that yours are not the worst problems; they carry the weight that you lend them.

Free yourself from complaining and spend more time pondering ways to persevere and be productive.

Never give in to *empty time,* for it gets filled up with boredom, discomfort or perturbation.

Whatever you do, do it well, with dedication.

Remember that you are human, that the process of acquiring conscientiousness is slow, and that you will gain certainty and clarity through continuous action.

✳

Interested in deciphering the enigmas of human behavior, Allan Kardec asked the Benefactors and Guides of Humanity, as set out in *The Spirits' Book*, Question No. 621:

Where is God's law written?

"In the conscience," they answered wisely.

Conscientiousness is a significant stage that you must attain, so that you may follow the path to becoming a pure spirit.[6]

---

[6] "These spirits have ascended through all of the degrees of the scale [order of spirits] and have freed themselves from all the impurities of matter. Having reached the highest perfection possible for created beings, they have no more trials of expiations to endure. Moreover, because they are no longer subject to reincarnation in perishable bodies, they live eternally in the heart of God... They are the messengers and ministers of God, whose orders they carry out to maintain universal harmony." Allan Kardec, *The Spirit's Book*, Ch. 1, #113.

2
KNOWLEDGE AND CONSCIENTIOUSNESS

Through a careful analysis of human behavior, Jung found that, in all people, there is a predominant belief in three factors essential to life: God, the survival of the soul after death, and beneficent action for others, as well as for oneself.

Varying in name, form of acceptance, philosophy and religious faith, these three principles are fundamental to sustaining the social group and individual happiness.

They are basic concepts that have supported ethics and philosophical thought, opening broader perspectives for integrating the individual into the social group.

These manifestations originate in the spiritual Self and are brought from the spirit world – its home prior to reincarnation. Therefore, Jung's concept of the collective archetype – which he drew upon in trying to explain the belief – instead of having arisen in the individual and having been transmitted to subsequent generations, has its causality in the spiritual origin of life, which remains in seed form in the process of evolution until it takes form and expression in the current consciousness.

Necessarily, over time, highly-evolved missionary spirits have taken these principles and developed them, appearing in various forms of beliefs and religions, with worship forms compatible with the cultural stage of each era, people and race.

To the degree that their deeper meanings are learned, they become divested of unnecessary formulas and become ethical behavior toward life, oneself and one's neighbor. They enable individuals to fully integrate with their Creator, themselves and others. Without this identification, happiness is impossible.

No one is really happy alone.

Voluntary exile and solitude are methods for mental, emotional and behavioral discipline. However, once the control of the will is achieved, its application in everyday life and human relationships will attest to its effectiveness and the results of the endeavor.

Untested experience is an ornament that cannot be trusted.

Unapplied knowledge is information ignorant of its purpose.

Human beings are sociable, bearers of the gregarious instinct in order to evolve in relationship with others wherever they may be. Without such interaction, their values are unknown and their resilience is weak.

The knowledge of immortality leads individuals to behave ethically toward their neighbor, doing everything according to the standard that comprises their ideal, and which they would like to receive in return.

In this sentiment of solidarity lies the challenging goal to be reached in their evolutionary process and self-enlightenment.

A whole host of projects appear when individuals' physical existence takes on meaning and purpose, which organic death does not interrupt in its constant phenomenon of molecular transformations.

The immortalist viewpoint provides an expansion of life's objectives since, once a certain level of values and achievements is reached, another appealing one appears, promoting further efforts that foster the determined candidate's continuous intellectual and moral growth.

Questions and troubling circumstances, arising in the social context as important and accounting for countless conflicts that cause unhappiness, give way to legitimate aspirations to plenitude, which are set above seemingly important trivial matters, mere frivolities, wastes of time and emotional resources. This is because the certainty of the Divine Causality and Its Justice promotes a real understanding of the contents in favor of one's own future, which begins at that point.

Therefore, rational, logical and emotional knowledge about God, the soul's survival, and the act of loving one's neighbor, gives individuals understanding about their humanity and their future, glorious destiny.

Allan Kardec, concerned about the issue of happiness, asked the high-order Mentors how to focus on it, and they answered in question 919 of *The Spirits' Book*:

What is the most effective means for improving ourselves in this life and for resisting the draw of evil?

"A sage of antiquity has told you: 'Know thyself.'"

3
BEHAVIOR AND CONSCIENCE

Careful studies of human behavior have shown that there are three biotypes representative of individuals in society.

The first biotype can be termed as *codependent*. It is made up of conditioned individuals, that is, those who set their goals according to circumstances other than their wishes. They do not experience the personal satisfaction that comes from striving for self-realization. Their aspirations are based on other people's possibilities, on circumstances, and they claim that they can only be happy if they are loved, if they take this trip, or have that job, etc. Their lack of self-confidence disrupts their health, they are often susceptible to cancer, and they have a higher death rate than the other two biotypes.

The second biotype is made up of *disgruntled individuals:* those who are angry about life; those who are *against* it. They are unstable and irritable by nature, self-destructive, and live under the constant constriction of irascibility. They say they feel unfulfilled, that nothing goes right for them; hence, they take it out on themselves, everyone and everything else. They are easy prey for nervous disorders that chafe and make them even more miserable, casting them into the dungeons of exaltation, depression and direct or indirect suicide...

Amongst these are despots, warriors, criminals…

The third group consists of *well-adjusted individuals:* those who are self-realized, calm, confident. There are not very many of them, of course, and they differ greatly from members of the other two groups. These well-adjusted people are candidates for success in the activities to which they dedicate themselves. They are pleasant, sociable and encouraging. Their endeavors are positive and always aimed at the common good, the progress of all. Their leadership is enriching, creative and dignified. This group produces promoters of social development, examples of sacrifice, creative geniuses, seekers of the Truth…

*

Studies have probed the proximate causes of these behaviors and have found the family group to be at their root.

With slight variations involving those who overcome negative factors and become well-adjusted, as well as others who, in spite of worthy support, lose their way, the home accounts for the future happiness or misery of the offspring, creating both good and bad individuals.

Those who do not receive love do not know how to give love because they have none to give.

In the infancy of the body, the incarnate spirit instills in its conscience the range of values that will guide its existence. Depending on how it is treated, it will follow in the same direction and will pay it back in kind.

Thus, self-esteem develops when the incarnate spirit is oriented toward meaningful discoveries about life, its own possibilities, and the latent qualities that must be developed.

Challenges are seen as invitations to strive, to toil for progress, to achieve goals. Failure neither phases nor discourages it, because it teaches it what not to do.

Affection, love and tenderness in childhood, alongside respect for the child, are fundamental for a healthy, wholesome life.

Everyone needs security on the transient and unstable incarnate journey. And parents, educators and adults in general are models for the child, who will love and copy them, or loathe and unconsciously embody them.

It is true that each spirit reincarnates into the home it needs in order to evolve, but this does not give the parents the right to be arbitrary, because they will have to give an accounting for it to the Cosmic Conscience, as well as their own.

The spirit reincarnates to progress by developing and improving the skills that sleep in its unconscious. Early childhood education plays a fundamentally important role for its behavior throughout life. Love helps it polish the rough edges left over from the past, through honorable conduct, solidarity, selflessness and charity.

With rare exceptions, the great figures of humanity possessed a greater behavioral awareness based on what was learned at home, and on the care of parents, grandparents and teachers, who became examples worthy of emulation. Their reminiscences were rich in beauty, kindness and love, which made them strong for the grand endeavors of existence, and those who were victims of supreme sacrifice were at peace for having died to benefit posterity.

Responding to Allan Kardec, question 918 of *The Spirits' Book*, the Guides of Earth asserted:

"The Spirit proves its progress when all the actions of its corporeal life consist in practicing the law of God, and when it understands the spirit life beforehand."

Behavior is therefore a result of an individual's level of conscientiousness.

4

Conflict and Conscientiousness

All the individual's processes of anthropological evolution and psychological acquisitions sleep in the depths of the unconscious in the form of experiences. Each time an experience could not be assimilated, it got stored in the deep archives of the unconscious. It remained there to probably emerge later as a conflict.

Conflicts also result from unfulfilled ambitions, frustrated desires and inner manifestations that were repressed without the help of reason.

When human beings emerge from the primal stages, they live temporarily on the border between instinct and discernment of what is feasible to accomplish.

Once they have become used to automatic phenomena, they do not always have the moral strength to overcome that limitation, from which arise uncertainties and doubts that become complex emotional conflicts.

Ingrained behaviors and insecurity lie buried in the unconscious, where they remain as tormenting impulses and perturbing complexes that promote the unhappiness of those who experience their constriction.

A conflict is the certainty/uncertainty about what to do or not do, which always causes imbalance and affliction.

Undigested, a conflict becomes an emotional expression of maladjustment, manifesting as organic dystonias that open the way for various diseases.

A vigorous *parasite,* the conflict must be identified and eliminated.

Every time something dark appears in the area of the emotions because of fear, ignorance, pressure or weakness, it may become a conflict later.

However, there is actual conflict only when the conscience does not possess the light of discernment; still in the dark, it lets itself be guided solely by the intelligence or instincts, and remains directionless.

Human existence is a constant challenge.

Every challenge requires effort for the struggle.

When individuals recoil from a trying experience, they lose the chance to affirm their values, at the expense of their personal growth.

Obstacles and hard-to-grasp concepts are skill-building tools. When the mind gets blocked, people stop moving forward, and they get lost in a tangle of fears and insecurities.

Therefore, they need to use logic in order to act, weigh the possibilities and produce, working for their inner growth, which is responsible for the psychophysical harmony of their evolutionary process.

Consciousness expands the horizons of thought, promoting real health, which is expressed as balance before the cosmos.

Since individuals are a miniature cosmos, the same Laws govern both.

This perfect concurrence between small focal points and the great Focal Point produces harmony, which is the universe's noblest manifestation.

✳

Conflicts that manifest in individuals' conduct and emotions are the effects of the incarnate spirit's level of evolution.

The body, molding itself to the subtle nature of the perispirit, reflects the need for progress, propelling the spirit toward incessant intellectual and moral transformation – its purpose, its quest.

Furthermore, given the history of their past lives, individuals still suffer conflicts that are suggested and transmitted to them by spirits who had been their followers or victims during such times.

Due to the notable and frequent manifestation of conflict in people's lives, Allan Kardec asked the Guardian Spirits for clarification in question 361 of *The Spirits' Book*:

Where do a person's good or bad moral qualities come from?

"They reflect the qualities of the incarnate spirit. The purer the spirit, the more the person is inclined toward the good." Which is to say, free of conflict.

Therefore, overcoming conflict occurs by means of enormous effort on the part of those who want to attain plenitude.

5
HEALTH AND
CONSCIENTIOUSNESS

In order for individuals to acquire or preserve their health, becoming aware of themselves and their manner of being is essential.

Usually, out of habit, they prefer and accept negative and altered behavioral states for the pleasure they bring, thus opening the way for illnesses. Consequently, they indulge in anger, jealousy, complaining and anxiety, and they lapse into depression, which is a gateway to various infirmities.

Always justifying perturbing thoughts and harmful actions, they refuse to renew their mental landscape with its consequent changes in attitude, thereby predisposing themselves to even more imbalance.

The warning signs regarding such a situation arise when one wants to:

Apologize for a wrongful reaction, but cannot do so;

Recommence a task that was interrupted by anger, but feels reluctant;

Embrace an unfriendly person, but finds it impossible;

Discuss an unpleasant subject, but is taken by an awkward silence;

Start a conversation, but feels incapable or uninterested...

Or when one:

Stays awake, unable to break free of an upsetting idea;

Continues to be anxious, even when there is no reason for it;

Feels unable to say something kind to a loved one;

Trembles or feels extremely uncomfortable in the presence of someone perceived as being superior;

Considers oneself unimportant within one's social environment...

These and other symptoms characterize states that predispose one to disease.

Accepting these circumstances points to a preference for unhappiness.

By cultivating these states, the conscience is blocked and becomes deadened. It returns to a lower level, to the sensations that still predominate in the evolutionary process.

*

Since people are free to choose to be healthy or sickly, it is up to them to act with real freedom and make the decision to be happy.

Start by undoing old, negative mental patterns, which have conditioned you to accept unhealthy behaviors.

By practicing new ways of thinking based on order, the general good, and the development of your own potential, you will create automatic reflexes that will produce harmony and health.

You must assume control of yourself, which is to say, become self-aware – that higher level at which emotion directs sensation.

Endless messages are directed from the mind to the body, producing habits that take root, replacing those that are responsible for disharmony and disease.

Your brain, with its extraordinary files, is always storing data, and has the ability to store ten new facts per second.

It may seem hard to leave a bad situation for a better one. And it really is. Even so, all learning requires the repetition of the experience until it becomes set. Similarly, the acquisition of values and standards of happiness goes beyond simply wanting. It is necessary to walk the path of achievement.

✳

Technology made its most significant leap in modern times when two young American scientists invented the transistor in 1948, miniaturizing parts and equipment, hence accelerating the progress of civilization.

Sparing no effort to acquire health through awareness of one's duty to oneself is the challenge one must face and overcome through small instances of sacrifice, perseverance and work.

In question 912 of *The Spirits' Book,* Allan Kardec asked:

What is the most effective means of fighting the predominance of the corporeal nature?

And the Spirit Mentors answered:

"Practicing self-denial."

With this effort you will enjoy conscientiousness, health and peace.

6
GUILT AND
CONSCIENTIOUSNESS

G uilt arises as a form of catharsis necessary for release
from conflicts.
It is engraved on the foundations of the spirit and
manifests either consciously or through complex mechanisms
of unconscious self-punishment.

Its roots may lie in a past life – hidden wrongs and
crimes that were not brought to justice – or in the recent
past, in actions involving impertinence or wrongdoing.

Generator of serious disorders, guilt must be released
so that the damage caused by it may disappear.

Regret for wrongful behaviors and for petty, selfish
and willful acts is perfectly normal. However, holding on
to regret is not only useless but harmful, which accounts for
numerous conflicts of the personality.

Regret is meant to make individuals realize the scale
of their offense, of their debt, so that they may become
aware of what they did and commit themselves to not have
a relapse. But continuously analyzing it and mulling over
what should or should not have been done becomes a thorn
in the conscience.

There are people who torment themselves with guilt about what they did not do; they regret not having enjoyed all that the past offered them. Others torment themselves due to the misuse or inadequate use of an opportunity. Both types, however, represent negative behavior.

＊

Whatever you did or did not do, holding on to the guilt of that moment will not help you at all.

You cannot erase the error by regretting it no matter how long you dwell on it, nor will you find relief by recalling what you could have done but did not do. As long as you proceed like that, the apparent compensation you may experience is neurotic because you return over and over again to the same memories, which will become a mental corrosive in the future.

Any attempt at cancelling out, erasing or pushing the past aside will be pointless.

What you have done or what is yet to be done are experiences for future behavior.

All that is water under the bridge, the popular aphorism states wisely.

Negative memories dampen one's enthusiasm for uplifting actions, the only means of hope for release from guilt.

There are small wrongs that result from a poor, neurotic education in the home. These are also perturbing, but are relatively unimportant.

＊

Taken as a whole, earthly existence is an opportunity for continuous enrichment.

Every moment is a chance for new activities to foster growth, knowledge, achievement. Knowing how to use it is a challenge for individuals who long for new accomplishments.

Thus, those who dwell in the gloomy landscapes of guilt have not yet realized their responsibility toward life, and they deny themselves the blessing of release.

In some ways, those who cultivate guilt do not even want release; they take irresponsible pleasure in such a posture.

Leave regret behind and act correctly and constructively.

Right the wrong through new actions that represent the current state of your soul.

Halt the wave of its harmful effects by diluting them on the new frontiers of the good.

The sum of your positive actions will pay your moral debt to the Divine Conscience, for the important thing is not to whom you have done something good or bad, but your action per se in relation to the universal harmony.

Allan Kardec asked the Spirit Ambassadors about the matter and received their sure response, according to question 835 of *The Spirits' Book:*

Is freedom of conscience a consequence of freedom of thought?

"Conscience is an inner thought that belongs to persons, as do all their other thoughts."

Consequently, guilt must be overcome through positive, rehabilitative actions, which will result from inner, ennobling thoughts.

7

MATURITY AND CONSCIENTIOUSNESS

Conscientiousness blossoms when individuals mature during the psychological process of evolution. This maturity is the result of continuous striving for self-knowledge and the courage to face oneself, working inwardly to overcome the limitations and infantile processes that still predominate.

Since they do not know how to overcome frustrations, they let them take root in the unconscious and become their victim, and they resort to the mechanisms of irresponsibility every time they find themselves grappling with difficulties and confrontations.

Psychological immaturity is not characteristic of the childhood developmental period only, but of the different stages of life, considering the fact that learning and growth never stop until the moment of individuation, when the spirit takes control of matter and the mental remains in harmony with the physical.

Hence, it is not surprising that adults may hold on to childish behaviors, whereas young people may demonstrate balanced maturity.

Of course, the spirit is the agent of life, and the values that are or are not considered during corporeal existence proceed from it.

Individuals' mechanism for psychological maturation is expressed in a natural way, awaiting their will and continuous effort to acknowledge their physical, emotional and other weaknesses, providing the motivation to correct and overcome them.

The psychic functions, which Jung classified as being four – sensory, emotional, intellectual and intuitive – should form a harmonious whole, without the predominance of one over the others, providing maturation, and, therefore, conscientiousness.

Psychological maturity is expressed when one loves, when one reaches that self-giving sentiment, showing liberation from infantilism.

Egocentric and ambitious, the child[7] clings to ownership and does not give; it demands to be protected but never protects, and it receives love but does not know how to love or how to express it. Its love is possessive and is always expressed in receiving, in taking. The child lives 100 percent in the present.

The adult,[8] on the other hand, understands that love is the science and art of giving, of bringing happiness to others.

Its time reference is the future, which the present builds step by step to the degree that affectivity and the psyche mature.

[7] The Jungian concept – Tr.
[8] Ibid – Tr.

As long as love does not feel the pleasure of giving, it is still in the infantile period, characterized by jealousy, insecurity, and unreasonable demands, and is thus self-centered, inappropriate.

Those who love in a mature manner are pleased with the happiness of their loved one, and they benefit from the pleasure of loving.

They have an understanding of freedom that reaches the pinnacles of personal selflessness on behalf of the loved one's joy and complete freedom.

What they cannot accomplish today, they sow in hope for tomorrow.

Mature elderly persons feel fulfilled through ongoing experiences of love and beneficent cultural, emotional, and social experiences, free of the past and meaningless memories.

Since mature individuals' growth never ends, their conscience gives them the certainty that, divested of the body, they will continue to evolve.

Summarizing all of His wisdom, Jesus, the Ultimate Psychologist, prescribed the need to love one another.

With that unparalleled lesson, He not only reformulated the egocentric proposals of the Old Law, of cruel and therefore childish reactions, but also opened up extraordinary perspectives for integrating individuals with their Creator – Love Supreme.

Later, seeking to help humans to mature, Allan Kardec asked the Messengers of Light: *Which is the most meritorious of all the virtues?* and they answered, as recorded in *The Spirits' Book,* in question 893:

"All virtues are meritorious because all are signs of progress on the path of the good. There is always virtue when there is voluntary resistance to the allure of wrongful tendencies. However, the highest virtue consists in the sacrifice of one's own interests for the good of one's neighbor without ulterior motives. The greatest merit is that which is based on the most disinterested charity." Thus, it is through self-knowledge that thinking individuals become aware of their own imperfections; they work on them, and, led by gregarious need, they exit loneliness and begin to love.

8
KARMA AND
CONSCIENTIOUSNESS

Karma is the effect of actions taken at different stages of the current existence as well as those of the past. *Fruit* of the planted and cultivated tree, karma has the flavor of the species that typifies the plant.

Positive acts produce excellent results, rewarding those responsible with happiness, affectivity, lucidity, progress and new opportunities for moral, spiritual, intellectual and human growth, promoting society as a whole.

But when individuals act with foolishness, vulgarity, perversion, rebelliousness, or hatefulness, they reap suffering down the road, in the form of trials and complex and afflictive expiations meant to set them straight.

Karma is an ever-changing process that depends on a person's behavior.

Ongoing misery, exasperating mental strictures, dreadful, maddening diseases, frustrating physical limitations, suffocating loneliness, embittering misfortunes – all these could change if individuals would only resolve to modify their attitudes, enhancing and developing them for the general good, and consequently their own.

In the sovereign Laws of Life, no one is destined for a life of misery and misfortune.

What happens to individuals is the result of what they did of their own free will. It is never something that God does to them, as the pessimists, the defeatists and the indolent would state.

Therefore, improve your life constantly through positive acts.

Create new karmic outcomes, freeing yourself from the painful ones that weigh on your moral economy.

*

Conscientiousness is not intelligence in the mental sense; it is the ability to set parameters for understanding good and evil, opting for the former, proceeding with balance, and taking into account all latent possibilities, developing one's current resources for the sake of one's process of becoming.

Such dormant resources are the presence of God in everyone, waiting for the time to bloom and grow.

The conscience, on its various levels, coalesces the programming of future events by which it evolves further.

While *asleep*, the conscience works through automatisms that extend from the instinct to the acquisition of reason. When *lucidity* promotes discernment, the more the divine qualities manifest, increasing one's ability to love and serve.

Karma derives from conscious conduct; thus it has the quality of the level of perception that typifies it.

Therefore, raise your conscientiousness, and your karma will be luminous and peaceful, leading you to your plenitude.

✳

While still ignorant, Mary Magdalene lived in moral promiscuity because her conscience was dormant. Upon meeting Jesus, it awakened, changing her behavior to such an extent that she created the blessed karma of being the first person to see Him risen.

Although Judas Iscariot was aware of the Master's mission, he poisoned himself with the vapors of misplaced ambition, and when he awakened later and hanged himself, he established the dismal karma of wretched reincarnations to repair his dark errors and recover.

Karma and conscientiousness go hand-in-hand, the former being the result of the latter.

Allan Kardec, in *The Spirits' Book*, question 132, asked: *What is the purpose of the incarnation of spirits?*

And the Messengers replied:

"God imposes incarnation for the purpose of leading spirits to perfection: for some, it is an expiation; for others, a mission. However, in order to reach this perfection, *they must undergo all the vicissitudes of corporeal existence* – therein lies their expiation. Incarnation has a further objective, which is to place spirits in situations where they can do their share in the work of creation."

9

DEATH AND CONSCIENTIOUSNESS

The complete identification of the transitory nature of the physical body testifies to the highest stage of human awareness. This understanding concerning the weakness of the body is highly significant in the evolutionary process, and comprises a high level of achievement that raises individuals from the level of the instincts to that of reason, and from reason to spiritual intuition.

Instinctual humans find remembering death to be repugnant, as well as living with it in daily life. For them, the physical body stage has a sense of permanence that numbs them to the knowledge of reality, which they refuse to accept, despite the constant biological phenomenon of cellular and molecular transformation.

The security of the organic edifice rests on the weakness of its own constitution.

Its delicate inner workings are susceptible to disruption, either by accidents involving its structure, by microbial invasions, by physical and emotional traumas, or simply by the normal wear and tear that results from its use over time.

Unconscious humans like to think only of the immediacy of the physical body and to enjoy the apparent benefits it provides in the area of the pleasures and highly aggressive sensations, which they delight in with insatiable eagerness.

This error causes them to become attached to forms that dissipate and change; to objects they own now, but then change hands; to aspirations that become goals in life and to which they yield, expressing them in power, prominence, and affluence, which they cannot hold on to forever.

The effect of this action unsupported by life's reality is that individuals develop anxiety, fear, insecurity and irritability. These degenerate into dynamics of unhappiness, because physical life becomes their only reason for being and they struggle and strive to hold on to it.

As they experience progressive functional decline, infirmity and old age, they sense that the end is near and they are thrown off balance.

Ignoring or being too stubborn to acknowledge the inevitable transformation that ends one cycle to give way to the emergence of another – whence they came – they rebel and poison themselves with anger, which only precipitates the very thing they want to put off.

✳

Conscientiousness reveals individuals' deepest reality, such that they comprehend the natural changes of the biological phenomena, which are tools for their spiritual progress.

No longer numbed by the atavistic anesthetics of the *preservation instinct*, anesthetics left over from animal primitivism, they delve into the structure of life and discover that its existential causality is the spirit, independent of the body, which they use for specific purposes and then leave behind when the activity it was needed for ends.

When they finally grasp that fact, they develop invaluable resources and discover latent attributes, opening themselves up to imperceptible qualities that captivate them to the detriment of others that may be needed for the physical journey, but which should stay on the earthly stage where they have originated.

Awareness about death, with the consequent, preparatory actions for the transition, provides these individuals with inner harmony and personal security.

Clarity about their duties drives them to work on self-improvement, and, in doing so, they discover that love is the inexhaustible fount of resources for the job.

Ever-expanding love frees them from enslaving, perturbing passions.

✳

If you are already aware of the proximity of death, which represents transformation in your life, you can grow and soar above vicissitudes.

Therefore, live the physical journey conscientiously, using your body for lofty purposes, for, at the moment of your death, you will leave its material mass behind like a blissful butterfly, which, after histogenesis, is happily swept away by the gentle rivers of the infinite.

In question 155 of *The Spirits' Book,* one reads:

How does the separation of the soul from the body occur?

"Once the bonds that held the soul are ruptured, it disengages itself."

With awareness of reality, life thrives in the body and out of it.

10
REINCARNATION AND CONSCIENTIOUSNESS

The lucid acquisition of conscientiousness makes room for understanding the laws that govern life, fostering individuals' progress as they strive for their own education and, therefore, that of society.

Their aspirations are no longer satisfied by the utopian concepts and childish statements devoid of reason that used to anesthetize the discernment of the masses.

With conscientiousness, the idea of God and His Justice evolves, releasing Him from the anthropomorphism, to which He used to be shackled due to ignorance, for a reality more in line with His greatness.

Old taboos, in effect, give way to facts that can be considered and examined through research, producing broad perceptions of content that enrich understanding.

Inner growth clarifies justice, which is no longer bound by the limits of the human passions that standardized it according to their own interests, blessing some and punishing others, in a regrettable ethical aberration and questionable, if not absurd, equanimity.

The acquisition of conscientiousness promotes the understanding of the causes of life through the processes of intuition, deduction, and analysis derived from experience in relation to the factors that constitute the universe.

Men and women who rid themselves of fear or disbelief, feigned devotion or denial, become great individuals and assume a dignified attitude, one consistent with their state of evolution.

Conscientiousness alone promotes perfect identification with the reality of successive lives, the sole concept-law that corresponds to the grandeur of life.

Without conscientiousness, the mind thinks logically and believes, but does not submit; emotion accepts, but fears the impositions of the statutes of evolution, in which reincarnation lies.

Conscientiousness opens the floodgates of the heart and mind to the natural acceptance of successive and inevitable lives, which promote the individual.

Reincarnation is the instrument for spiritual progress. At times, individuals must endure expiation when their wrongs are serious, submitting to afflictions that are educational disciplines, whereby the duties they must fulfill are fixed deep in their conscience. At other times, they undergo trials, which strengthen the moral fibers responsible for dignifying action.

Rather than being a punishment, the gift of physical rebirth is a blessing of God's love. It helps the spirit develop latent resources, like soil that is tilled and fertilized so that the tiny seed may become the lush plant sleeping within...

Given this reality, broaden your conscientiousness through reflection and act with ethical certainty, surrendering from now on to the duty of enlightenment.

Never put off your duties under the pretext that you will have future opportunities.

Your conscience will tell you that today, here and now, is the time and the place to build your spiritual Self, which must ascend, freeing itself from primitive atavisms and perturbing passions.

Awareness of reincarnation will drive you to progress through love and the good with no alternative for failure, because the light of happiness shining ahead will be the stimulus for reaching your goal.

Without reincarnation, intelligent life would return to chaos and the logic of progress would be reduced to stupidity and ignorance.

∗

The awareness of reincarnation explains Socrates contrasted with the barbaric human of his time; Gandhi, with today's primitive; and civilization, with today's lingering primitivism…

Individuals progress slowly and, step-by-step, they acquire experience, knowledge, sentiment, wisdom, and conscientiousness.

In question 170 of *The Spirits' Book*, we find the following dialog:

What does the spirit become after its final incarnation?

"A blessed spirit; a pure spirit."

For that desired goal, the awareness of reincarnation is indispensable.

11
CONSCIENTIOUSNESS
AND EVOLUTION

The awakening to conscientiousness promotes responsibility for one's acts, due to the blossoming of the Divine Codes that lie in seed form within the individual.

Created *simple and ignorant,* the spirit is destined for perfection. Attaining it quickly or slowly depends on its own desire and free will.

Having passed through the die of ignorance, it acquires experiences by which it can discern between what it should and should not do, opting for actions that bring about happiness and well-being, without harmful effects, those that become stressful and afflicting.

In this way it becomes responsible for its destiny, which it is building and modifying by means of its decisions and attitudes.

Its guiding light is the good, constituted of *all that conforms to God's laws,* which are natural and in force everywhere.

The inheritance of primitive ignorance attaches the spirit to evil, which is contrary to the *Law of Progress.* Nonetheless, such inheritance does not hold it and keep it from being happy indefinitely.

Thus, individuals should strive to break the bonds that hold them back, advancing by means of illuminative experiences, at first with difficulty, given their conditioning, and then more quickly, by force of the resulting pleasure and joy.

Slowly, due to their own awareness, they discover the invaluable treasures available to them and which may be used with endless benefits.

Health and illness, peace and conflict, joy and sorrow may be chosen through the discernment that guides their actions. Without this light, negative states become the well-established norm, but even then, endeavoring to overcome them may alter them.

Never give in to despair or surrender. You are not a rolling stone on the bed of the river of fate. You have a goal that awaits you and you will reach it.

Through deep reflection, you will uncover your incalculable potential for self-realization.

Affirm yourself in the good so that its seed may be fertilized and grow within you. You will be what you think and plan for, since the qualities you cultivate proceed from your heart and mind.

Your natural state is health. Infirmities are *bumps in the road,* resulting from negative actions, providing for your rehabilitation. It is essential that you remain alert and watchful regarding the way you use your physical vessel. So, think in terms of well-being; yearn for it and induce it by acting correctly.

Your constitution is harmonious. Imbalances are instances in the electric current of the nervous system due to the distortion of the charge fostered by cultivated sensations. Keep the vigilance switch turned on so that it may prevent the high voltage that produces such distortions.

At your origin you are light evolving toward the Great Light. There is darkness only because you have not yet decided to set in motion the mighty power generators of energy asleep within you. Turn on the light, starting with the spark of good will, letting it grow to reach maximum power.

Love is your pathway because it comes from God, who created you. Thus, allow your aspirations to embrace the vertical life and expand your sentiments in the direction of the First Cause.

You can do anything if you want to.

You will succeed if you put your mind to it.

✳

Seeking to grasp the order of the Divine Laws that provide an understanding of life, Allan Kardec asked the Venerable Spirits, as recorded in question 117 of *The Spirits' Book:*

Does it depend on spirits themselves to hasten their advancement toward perfection?

"Absolutely. The amount of time it takes them depends on their desire and submission to God's will. Doesn't a well-behaved child learn faster than one who is obstinate?"

12

CONSCIENTIOUSNESS
AND HABITS

St. John of the Cross stated that God is found in the darkness of the human being.

That innate, profound Self of individuals' yet-undetected reality lies in their *dark side.*

As long as this area of *shadows* has not been lit by reason, ignorance prevails and the instincts rule, even if reasoning seems to control their habits and actions.

Effort must be continuously exerted in every period of earthly existence, because experiences are what raise individuals to more significant levels, offering more ample opportunities for self-knowledge.

The roots of the individual are Divine, making the body an instrument or fertile soil for the unfolding of latent treasures.

Of course, endogenous factors such as heredity, the endocrine system,[9] and others, weigh on individuals' shoulders on the long human journey, as do exogenous factors, such as the contributions of education, society and/

9 The bodily system that consists of the endocrine glands and the hormones they secrete. http://medical-dictionary.thefreedictionary.com/ endocrinal . – Tr.

or the economy as generators of habits. However, it is the spirit, heir to its own achievements, which transfers from one existence to the next, acquisitions that advance it, retain it, or trap it in perturbing states.

Given the habit of instant satisfaction, down through time a fissure has opened up between the superficial and deep consciousness, developing the areas of the personality at the expense of the areas of the individuality.

This separation has caused individuals to be disinterested in transcendental achievements, which seem too difficult or discouraging, such is the preoccupation with the physical aspect of life.

Confirming that statement, science discovered that the human brain's left hemisphere, in charge of reflexes on the right side of the body, is verbal, relative, angular, individual and developed, whereas the right hemisphere, responsible for the left side of the body, is global, intuitive, quiet, selective and little used, and is therefore undeveloped, waiting for the mind, in its legitimate function, to foster the enrichment of its abilities and achievements.

The mind per se, the spirit, uses the brain to manifest itself in two different ways: at times as reason – intuitive, metaphysical, abstract – and at other times as intelligence – concrete, analytical, immediate.

The use of reason provides discernment, which fosters choosing healthy habits conducive to happiness, emulators of evolution.

*

The mind's function is to think.

The habit of thinking expands the potential to discern.

The mind is capable of using reason to recognize its own errors and correct them.

Laziness regarding thinking is responsible for limiting one's discernment, one's reason.

Conforming to narrow and superficial analyses of life and its manifestations, individuals remain at a lower stage, squandering time and opportunities.

The endeavor to maintain attention – which observes; concentration – which assimilates; and deep reflection – which completes the psychophysical balance becomes the bridge of union between the surface conscious and the deep Self, thus unifying the activities of the two brain hemispheres, which become harmonized and develop in tandem.

The repetition of acts generates habits and these become memories that begin to function automatically.

If you choose mental habits of discernment for what is correct, you will act with confidence, and those *memories* will function automatically, maturing you intellectually and emotionally, and this behavior will give you self-awareness, oneness with your deep Self.

✳

"The Kingdom of Heaven is within you," emphasized Jesus with infinite wisdom and with an extraordinary relevance of content during an age of great ignorance.

Depth psychology today reveals that dark side of individuals, illuminating them with the presence of the spirit in the body, such as the contribution proposed by Viktor

Frankl in his *noetic* approach, a word derived from the Greek word *nous* or spirit.

Allan Kardec, the Missionary of the New Era, shedding light on the dark instances of the sleeping human conscience, after questioning the Instructors of Humanity about progress, received the comforting and sure answer from them, according to question 779 of *The Spirits' Book:*

"They [humans] advance naturally by themselves. Not all progress at the same time or in the same manner, however, and it is through social contact that the most advanced help the others to progress."

13
CONSCIENTIOUSNESS
AND DISCERNMENT

In classical antiquity, the Greeks explained that *human beings are rational animals and that, to achieve full development, they should use reason.*

The acquisition of reason, however, takes place through efforts exerted by the mind, by an orderly approach.

The mind can become a heaven or a hell, depending on the direction given to one's thought.

The cultivation of ideas derived from the lower passions causes disorders that alienate and brutalize, hindering the prevalence of discernment.

Discernment results from practicing the art of thinking, which should grow properly, providing the individual with the perception of being and non-being, of right and wrong, of what is just and what is abominable.

Two propositions emerge as the correct methodology for the development of reason, for the use of discernment: the act of always thinking and what to think about.

In the first case, one requires education by means of constant thinking, since its function develops the centers through which it manifests, consequently increasing the ability to always think.

It is essential to combat mental laziness, that generator of inattention, torpor and difficulty in concentrating.

Electing the kind of thoughts to cultivate is a highly important step for discernment to manifest conscientiousness in the choosing of the codes of behavior that will be incorporated into one's life...

It is said that no one can live without thinking, but that statement is misconstrued. All those in the first stages of evolution think very little or almost not at all.

Victims of impulses of their *animal nature*, they let themselves be dragged along by tendencies and instincts until that compulsory moment when they become enlightened by reason, driving them to examine events and behavior.

Others, who have already reached this stage but still lack the habit of thinking, allow themselves to be numbed and accept facts and existential phenomena without intelligent incentives for reaching higher levels.

Discernment brings thinking individuals psychological maturity and, by extension, emotional maturity. Therefore, they discover their own importance in their social group and strive to fulfill their duties.

It broadens their horizon of human understanding, and an all-encompassing love for everything and everyone fills their hearts, giving them the existential conscientiousness responsible for healthy behavior, which promotes happiness.

This discerning conscientiousness facilitates the intuition about life's transcendence, expanding the potential for intellectual-moral development, aimed at the infinite of relative perfection.

Thus, the acquisition of discernment and conscientiousness blesses the human being with plenitude, longed for by martyrs and apostles, by saints and sages of all times, in all cultures...

✳

As it passes through the die of reincarnations, the spirit develops the higher qualities that lie in seed state and, in contact with the experiences of reason, provides the conditions for that development, dignifying their owners and encouraging their self-realization – the goal of rebirths, the objective for which we were all created.

Allan Kardec reflects on the subject, according to question 189 of *The Spirits' Book*:

From the time it is first formed, does a spirit enjoy the fullness of its faculties?

"No. Like a human being, a spirit has its infancy. When they first come into being, spirits have no more than an instinctive existence, possessing only the consciousness of themselves and their actions. Their intelligence only develops little by little."

The development of the intelligence and sentiment gives rise to conscientiousness, to discernment.

14
CONSCIENTIOUSNESS AND DUTY

Due to the fanciful nature of the plans that people make, their priorities are far from the spiritual reality. Instant gratification prevails, thus determining their behavior.

Although they recognize the impermanence of physical life and all that concerns it, they cling to transient events and phenomena, trying to eternalize them in time, which elapses, and in their emotions, which dwindle as a result of the inevitable changes in the somatic body.

As a consequence, they wear themselves out in a constant struggle to hold on to what is perishable and the search for new goals. They neglect self-realization, which stems from a lucid conscience marking victory over itself.

Due to atavism, they believe that the preservation of the species and the need to maintain the provisions necessary for that purpose are the objectives of life on earth. And without broader reflection they automatically set out to acquire things and money, social status and personal enjoyment. Their emotional range is restricted, which generates, with time and repetition, serious neuroses that drive them to spectacular escapes from reality, to conflicts and to the worst kinds of suffering...

Human beings are what they think about, what they make of themselves, building, through thought, their inescapable reality. Over time, their innermost aspirations materialize and surprise them, sometimes unexpectedly, for there is a time to sow and another to harvest.

*

Of course, success depends on a person's commitment. However, a goal, a plan and a strategy are indispensable.

The idea, plain and simple, needs a garb in order to be expressed, and the way in which it is presented accounts for its results.

Thus, words spoken cannot be taken back – they must follow their course. What they accomplish becomes the property of the one who uttered them.

The lucid conscience remains on guard in order not to create conflicts and suffering for itself by emitting negative concepts and taking harmful action.

Knowing their duties, individuals take responsibility by using opportunities to further develop their inborn potential, expanding their perception.

Conscientiousness in connection with duty is not the result of mythological archetypes, but of the moral achievements that promote individuals, releasing them from *aggressive instincts, libido,* and feral passions.

One can measure people's level of evolution by their conscientiousness in relation to duty. Its absence points to an elementary level, even if there are intellectual achievements, while its presence reveals the entire process of having stored up ethical and moral values.

Intelligence reflects the efforts that are externalized by the brain, while conscientiousness emanates from the folds of the spirit.

✳

Make of your earthly existence a heritage of eternal blessings.

Good habits, equanimity and a strong sense of duty will be with you to provide you with stimuli and new achievements, such that fatigue, boredom and bitterness may not find resonance in your sentiments and dispositions.

Each difficulty and problem will present you with a challenge, and if you get discouraged, heed St. Augustine's advice, as stated in the beautiful communication in *The Spirits' Book*, in his comments to question 919:

"Do what I used to do when I was living on the earth. At the end of each day, I examined my conscience, reviewed what I had done and asked myself whether or not I had failed to fulfill some duty and whether or not anyone might have had reason to complain about me. It was thus that I arrived at knowing myself and at seeing what there was in me that needed to be reformed..."

15
CONSCIENTIOUSNESS AND CHARACTER

Choosing ethical and moral values and determining life's goals, as well as the qualities that establish an individual's character, depict the emergence of conscientiousness. Its validity and development result from repeated episodes, accruing gains that enable the spirit to progress without long stays in the provinces of suffering: the legacy of ignorance.

Every achievement that is pondered, felt and cultivated produces a memory, which registers the strongest impressions.

People should concern themselves – in the good sense – with positive emotions and events in order to store up memories that act as stimuli for personal growth and harmony.

However, harried by fear and habitual pessimism, which expects continuous misfortunes, they soon forget about joyous times but dwell on disappointments.

Invited to adhere to standards of well-being, they eagerly seek self-punishment, utilizing masochistic means to inspire compassion, when they have invaluable resources that would foster and awaken love.

Due to their systematic unconsciousness, they refuse the rapture of light, beauty, and the meaning of life, surrendering to the vagaries of rebelliousness, that beloved child of disgruntled selfishness.

Believing they deserve to have it all, they attribute merits to themselves that they do not actually possess and refuse to acquire.

They compare themselves with people at other levels, without considering these people's sacrifices or even how they feel, establishing concepts of happiness based on a mere perception.

This is a leftover from the primitive instinctive stage prior to the emergence of reason.

They are shackled by atavisms from which they must break free, and they stifle the possibilities that would enable them to soar on the heights of sentiment and reason. The alternative of misery and a dysfunctional conscience becomes inevitable, generating behavior that leads to alienation.

Conscientiousness is an enlightening achievement. Preserving it results from the very effort that shapes the individual's character.

All individuals go down the same paths and experience similar challenges. With each test, people are promoted or held back for the fixation of the learning experience. Thus, progress is personal and non-transferable, in keeping with the Law of Justice and equanimity.

Each person ascends by means of self-abnegation.

✳

Hold your moments of joy in your memory, no matter how insignificant they may be. Their succession will give you an enormous store of stimulating emotions for the good.

Forget your failures after you consider the useful results you can draw from them.

When something good and positive happens to you, comment on it without fanfare; relive it and let yourself be gripped by its uplifting significance.

When you are visited by bitterness, disillusionment, pain or disappointment, seek to overcome it and carry on in search of new relationships; avoid harboring resentment and unhappy details.

Do not persist in making disagreeable comments – they invariably ooze unhappiness.

Out of unhealthy habit, people fixate on unhealthy occurrences and forget about healthy memories. Consequently, they lose their best memories and accumulate perturbing ones, which occupy their mental and emotional space, blocking the broad areas of development of the conscience.

Episodes of conscientiousness, whether minor or major, form the character that is the main line of conduct for life.

Conscientiousness can discover the most insignificant values and turn them into positive stimuli for other achievements.

The decision and effort to reach new evolutionary goals develop people's moral character, without which the most appropriately prepared plans for triumph fail.

The healthy, disciplined and responsible character defines individuals of the good, true prototypes that do not stop or give up when obstacles arise, threatening to make their progress difficult.

You must carry on with your plans for moral and spiritual development, as recorded by your conscience.

Do not surrender to indolence or rely on evasive or irrelevant reasons.

Once you have identified your duty, rush in and fulfill it.

Truly concerned about the progress of the spirit, Allan Kardec asked the High-Order Mentors, according to question 674 of *The Spirits' Book*:

Is the necessity of labor a law of nature?

"Labor is a law of nature, and as such is a necessity per se. Because civilization both increases peoples' needs and their enjoyments, it obliges them to work more."

16
CONSCIENTIOUSNESS AND RESPONSIBILITY

Responsibility is evidence for the acquisition of conscientiousness.

The act of thinking does not always foster the correct vision necessary for responsibility. Responsibility is based on the discernment of the objectives of earthly existence, driving the individual to ennobling actions along the lines of dignity.

Responsibility promotes the selection of duties, choosing those that are essential rather than those that may seem beneficial, but which are nothing but support for the mask of illusion and pleasure.

The responsible individual discerns what to accomplish and how to go about it.

The tendency to the good is innate in humans due to their Divine Origin. Carnal numbness sometimes blocks the ability to choose what conscientiousness suggests.

As a result, lucid individuals act wisely, relying on the forthcoming results without worrying about immediacy, knowing that the seed of light always produces clarity.

The state of unawareness in which many individuals linger is responsible for their prevailing aggressiveness and ignorance.

The responsibility brought forth by conscientiousness promotes individuals to a level of lucidity that leads them to aspire to the heights of evolution, which they start to seek with ardent devotion.

✳

Conscientiousness regarding responsibility will lead you:
Never to curse the marsh, but drain it instead;
Not to cultivate problems, but solve them instead;
Not to erect barriers that hinder your progress, but rather a bridge that will facilitate it;
Not to expect success without work. The former precedes the latter only in the dictionary;
Not to look emotionally downward to the dust and mud, but upward to the blazing stars;
Not to give up the struggle and thus lose the battle that never took place, but persevere to the end, because hope is the light that shines up ahead, pointing out the path to victory;
Not to speak ill of others, since you have your own shortcomings; instead, offer them words of encouragement;
Not to become upset because of misunderstandings, but feel alive and therefore vulnerable to the phenomena of the human journey.
Never plan on peace without having the requisites to cultivate it within; nevertheless, radiate the joy of the good, which fosters harmony.
Responsibility is not conducive to self-pity, presumptuousness, moral weakness, violence, lust for vile desires, or numbing pleasures...

Responsibility is creative and enriching because it entails ascension and growth.

✳

Louis Pasteur, opposed by scholars of his time, responsibly continued his discoveries of microbes, rabies prophylaxis, anthrax and all types of contagious diseases...

Kepler, persecuted, but aware of the charts of the heavens, persisted until he could present a remarkable theory about the planet Mars and formulate other laws that honor his name.

Hansen responsibly delved into his research until he managed to isolate the leprosy bacillus, saving millions of lives.

Copernicus, anathematized, responsibly demonstrated the two-fold movement of the planets and the heliocentric system, paying a high price for his audacious awareness.

The Curies responsibly engaged in tiresome experiments that opened new horizons for knowledge about radioactive materials.

Responsibility is a step on the ladder of conscientiousness; it fulfills men and women in all situations.

Given this reality, Allan Kardec asked the Spirits Benefactors, as set out in *The Spirits' Book*, question 780:

Does moral progress always follow intellectual progress?

"It is its consequence, but it does not always follow it immediately."

It obviously depends on one's conscientiousness of responsibility.

.

17
CONSCIENTIOUSNESS AND INTEGRITY

Individuals who seek integrity – that state of complete moral balance – have acquired self-awareness, and have achieved the psychological maturity resulting from the correct observance of the Laws of Life.

Life is composed of the successive stages of the evolutionary process by which the spirit advances from one experience to the next, molding the inner pure spirit that sleeps in latency, the manifestation of divine consciousness, its origin, its causality.

On their journey, individuals normally get used to the amenities of the flesh either because of still-prevailing animal atavisms or because of self-indulgence, without realizing their urgent need for growth.

Every instance of development breaks such bonds, providing liberation and sometimes causing pain.

But seeking to escape pain, individuals usually turn to pleasure as a psychodynamic of evasion, and they begin to depend on it, thus programming inevitable future suffering.

Only awareness about life's overall goals fosters a correct vision for behavior that prepares one for the next step in a future reincarnation.

This results in the phenomena that show up in the area of behavior and, with them, one's tendencies, inclinations, aspirations, temperament...

Integrity arises from disciplining negative tendencies and superficial aspirations for the sake of deep values and full conscientiousness of life's objective and meaning.

*

If you wish to have the integrity of an individual of the good, start working on minor responsibilities and modest achievements.

It is too easy to become a giant in large and impressive accomplishments.

Real winners, however, become giants in the little things, ennobling themselves in insignificant tasks, without which massive constructions crumble and complex projects are rendered impracticable.

Such workers make themselves invisible in prominent situations but rise to the occasion in seemingly menial tasks.

They are not noticed when present, for everyone is used to their balanced demeanor and the harmony that surrounds them; however, when they are not present, everyone notices their absence and understands their value.

Individuals of integrity are true to their duty and never desert it. They are aware of its edifying power, and consequently, they are responsible, discreet and hardworking.

Whenever individuals seek new sensations to please the *ego*, they have not yet acquired the conscientiousness of integrity.

✳

The triumph of human beings over themselves is difficult, because it derives from living according to the good and order after the onset and subsequent action of lucid conscientiousness.

With extraordinary capacity for discernment, Allan Kardec molded his conscientiousness, applying to his own behavior the lessons he received from the Spirits and, establishing the basic guidelines for integrity, he defined them in individuals of the good as bearers of excellent qualities of heart, mind and character, taking Jesus as the model, according to question 625 of The Spirits' Book:

What is the perfect standard that God has offered to humankind as a guide and model?

"Jesus," answered the Wise Instructors from the Greater World, leaving us the epitome of conscientiousness and integrity.

18

CONSCIENTIOUSNESS AND MENTAL ALIENATIONS

The conscience is found in individuals at every stage of their evolution.

In the earliest stages, it manifests as flashes of discernment that drive them to reach higher levels.

Despite the predominance of aggressive instincts, sometimes flashes of conscientiousness arise and brighten the stormy night of impulses, expanding the horizons of perception.

Later, as reason develops, the conscientiousness expands and may become a victim of evasive mechanisms of cunning and the intellect, which numb it, harm it or poison it with the pernicious vapors of emotional aloofness.

Even so, conscientiousness breaks through the barriers and glimmers, making way for discernment and conflicts arising from its identification of wrongful acts.

Only when individuals go beyond the primary stages, when experiences become more significant through an understanding of the lofty meaning of life, does it fully manifest and begins to control the direction of existence, revealing itself victorious.

The conscience is the inner referee in charge of setting sure guidelines for one's life.

Varying in lucidity according to its stage of development, only when it becomes levelheaded can it lead the individual wisely.

As long as it is severe, demanding harsh reparations for wrongs, it dwells in the primitivism of revenge.

If, on the other hand, it is benign with respect to wrongs, it lacks the maturity that enables individuals to strive for higher purposes.

The conscience glows when, reflecting the Laws of God, it guides individuals toward the good, happiness, and peaceful progress in a climate of faith and hope.

The ennobled conscience establishes the regime for reparation and evolution based on the Laws of Love, always supported on Truth and Justice.

✳

In the deep psychogenesis of mental alienations lies the guilty conscience, the cause of torments that manifest as processes of reconstruction, recomposing the panels of duty by means of the painful mechanisms of mental disorder.

The breakdown of the mind provides the spirit with unsuspected suffering as a rigorous way to appease the conscience.

Since humans are the authors of their moral reality through their chosen behavior in the course of corporeal existences, at each step they prepare the method for their inner growth by means of their actions.

When they fail morally, they engrave with fire the means for reparation in their deep makeup, particularly in the area of the mind.

When unfortunate actions were undetected by human justice, the conscience, which is cognizant, disarranges the complex mechanisms of the unbalanced mind, which only expunging pain can recompose.

Within the context of mental alienations, whether in known, academically- studied psychopathologies, or in severe obsessions, it is the guilty conscience that facilitates the installation of the illness, which is expressed most rigorously during the process of readjustment and rebalancing.

A levelheaded conscience is maintained with good thoughts and reflection, which are the available, invaluable means for individuals to evolve.

A lucid and clear conscience is the best therapist for mental alienations, which is why all patients in need of health should not shirk the Herculean task of self-pacification, using prayer, deep reflection, self-knowledge and ennobling actions, all of which are conducive to a peaceful conscience, responsible for achieving progress.

In question 834 of *The Spirits' Book,* Allan Kardec asks: *Are humans responsible for their thoughts?*

"They are responsible before God. God alone can know their thoughts and condemn or absolve them according to divine justice."

Mental alienations are, therefore, *God condemning* the wrongful thoughts and actions of the primitive and mistaken conscience.

19
CONSCIENTIOUSNESS
AND MEDIUMSHIP

In the complex mechanism of human consciousness, the paranormal unfolds, broadening the horizons of perception concerning the deeper realities of the individual and life.

Erupting with relative violence in certain individuals with various ensuing disturbances, paranormality appears subtly in others, granting entrance into wider vibratory bands, those from where humans come before uniting with the body and to whose circle they return after the physical body has been depleted.

Manifesting as the soul's perception of the world that surrounds it, paranormality receives and transmits impressions that offer more stability to life's situations.

In addition to the manifestations peculiar to its attributes, it allows for mediumistic interaction with discarnate individuals, and this provides a complete view and full understanding of the dynamics of bodily existence and eternal reality.

At first, mediumship appears as strange sensations from somewhat disturbing psychic or physical presences, generating fear or anxiety, restlessness or uncertainty. At times, it creates confusion, whereas at others it opens luminous breaches in the mind, allowing for the perception of another, more subtle type of reality.

As the capabilities of inner silence and the reception of delicate interferences develop, the more the paraphysical realm asserts itself, proving to be the agent of occurrences on the sensory plane.

Mediumship, which lies latent in the human body, improves as one becomes aware of one's responsibility and the attention that the exercise of its well-directed function grants it.

A faculty of the higher consciousness or immortal spirit, it is clothed by the physical organs that externalize its phenomena in the world of concrete manifestations.

Mediumship is not symptomatic of evolution, sometimes comprising a path of expiatory afflictions for the specific purpose of inviting individuals to make a moral adjustment before the sovereign *Laws of God*.

When one conscientiously identifies mediumship's superior purpose and resolves to incorporate it into one's daily life, there is immense potential for achievement and unsuspected growth.

Mediumship is an invaluable bridge that unifies the hemispheres of physical life and death, eliminating distance and filling the gap between both.

Through it pass the liberating energies of knowledge, love and reason. But when uncontrolled, it promotes grudges, revenge and affliction.

Conscientiousness regarding one's spiritual reality provides an area of endless development that everyone can achieve.

∗

If you register the psychic presence of discarnate beings, or if you feel bound to baseless emotional afflictions, silence your unrest and go within via meditation.

Pray first. And probe your conscience.

Strive to develop your psychic awareness without any fear and you will perceive your loved ones approaching you.

You are not a static, finished reality.

In the process of your evolution, mediumship is a new field to winnow, awaiting the plow of your attention.

Mediumship is not a privilege; it is a fascinating acquisition for further growth and improvement of your tasks in the world.

Through it you will experience blissful landscapes, fulfilling interactions, and moments of profound reflection. Perhaps, on some occasions, you will be taken to sites of suffering and to distressed people who are also part of the evolutionary context.

You will tune in to pain, however, so that your desire to help others may awaken, gaining a better understanding of the Laws of Cause and Effect that govern the universe.

At other times, in uplifting moments, you will acquire wisdom and enlightenment for never-ending growth, leading along with yourself those who have not yet managed to walk without support.

In order to be dignified, mediumship needs the light of an ennobled conscience.

The greater the conscience's discernment, the broader the potential for mediumistic exchange.

✳

Before studying mediumship in greater depth, Allan Kardec asked the Messengers of Light, as recorded in question 408 of *The Spirits' Book*:

Sometimes it seems to us that we hear within us distinctly pronounced words that have no relation to what we are preoccupied with. Where do they come from?

The High-Order Spirits explained:

"Yes, and even entire sentences, especially when the senses begin to grow dull. It is sometimes the faint echo of a spirit who wishes to communicate with you."

Aware that this rich mediumistic potential is within your reach, become inwardly silent, study your faculty and, while meditating, get in tune with your spirit guide so that it may lead you surely, enlightening and strengthening your conscience.

20
CONSCIENTIOUSNESS AND PLENITUDE

The pursuit of plenitude is the essential goal of lucid conscientiousness that has discovered the real values of life and has overcome the errors of the *ego* in the process of the spirit's evolution.

Having become aware of the reality of life as being the Divine and Eternal Breath, the spirit knows that the brevity of life in the body in no way affects the content of what comprises it, for it understands the mechanism of evolution, thanks to which it enters the physical existence through fetal conception, and leaves it through cerebral anoxia at death.

Blessed with the complete identification of human goals, the spirit undertakes to store up the inalienable resources of the good, preserving its inner peace and behaving according to the canons of order and duty, those that promote individual, as well as overall progress.

Conscientiousness selects real needs from those that are utopian, making way for the self-realization that leads to love as a special means of achieving plenitude.

Dreamed of by all cultures throughout history, self-realization has been defined by saints, mystics and heroes as *Nirvana, Samadhi, Paradise* or *Glory,* finding in Jesus the lovely name *Kingdom of Heaven*, uncorrupted by pain or anguish, longings or afflictions.

Locating that Kingdom in the very heart of the individual, the Divine Master proposed immersion in the *ocean* of the sentiments, enjoying harmony, without anxiety, regret, disruption or torment...

Having attained conscientiousness, which provides maturation, individuals reach the state of spiritual plenitude, despite still being incarnate.

*

Fear neither death nor life.

Live in such a way that, before your discarnation, you may find yourself at peace, experiencing the biological phenomenon with the ease of someone who falls asleep with the unconscious certainty of awakening.

No expectations, no anxiousness.

Prepare to relocate from the organic plane to the spirit plane with secure tranquility.

While you are in the bodily life, cultivate fraternity, not letting yourself be troubled by quarrels and disruptive passions.

Live the hours of your existence intensely, tirelessly and really productively so that their memory may not cause you regret or lamentation.

Sometimes, a few minutes in the body are definers of an auspicious future due to the clarity of conscience for identifying wrongs and assimilating fulfilling achievements.

Moments of profound, objective awareness provide the memory of plenitude, the first step toward integration into the complete spirit of life.

✳

Jesus pointed to this achievement saying: "My Father and I are one."

There was a perfect oneness between Him and the Universal Creator, beckoning His disciples to the possibility of full consciousness with personal plenitude.

Interested in understanding plenitude, Allan Kardec asked the Spirits, as noted in *The Spirits' Book*, question 967:

What does the happiness of good spirits consist of?

"In knowing all things; in feeling no hatred, jealousy, envy, ambition or any of the passions that make people unhappy. The love that unites them is a source of supreme happiness. They do not experience the needs, sufferings or anxieties of material life. They are happy with the good they do…"